Advance Praise for Ann Eichenmuller's

The Writing Rx

While this book offers an impressive review of the research that shows the value of writing for our mental, emotional and spiritual well-being, perhaps more significantly, it offers us the wisdom of a seasoned teacher who knows how important it is that we each find our own way and our own voice.

While *The Writing RX* has a useful glossary of terms and includes discussions of forms and styles of writing, its purpose is to invite us to write. Using language and words, Eichenmuller shows us, is not only as sweet an experience as savoring your favorite chocolate, it also offers what e.e. cummings has called "the most wonderful life on earth." No matter what your current relationship with writing and language is, this book will nurture and encourage you.

Michael Glaser, PhD, Poet Laureate of Maryland, 2004-2009

Reading Ann's book is like having a conversation with a warm, intelligent friend. (Excuse me, I've never met the author so should be addressing her by her proper surname; but as I said, her writing is so friendly I forget formal etiquette.) *The Writing Prescription* is as much personal accounts of how writing helped her cope with various losses and difficulties as it is a how-to guide that each of us use to do the same. Who among us has not known trials and tribulations as we navigate life? The personal anecdotes she describes elicit memories of the reader's own experiences, making it so easy to relate to her.

Eichenmuller is quick to acknowledge that her approach is no substitute for medical treatment or psychotherapy, but rather an adjunct, a supplement that is available to all with merely pen and paper. While she tells us that writing is not magic, by the time you follow her guidance, something magical surely will follow!

Subtitled *Using the Healing Power of Writing for a Happier, Healthier Life*, the author talks about the pursuit of happiness, finding your own voice, indeed, gaining insight into your true self. These issues have been addressed by ancient philosophers and modern day gurus (and she quotes several of these sages). Yet, Ann offers some simple yet effective ways that just about anyone can take to explore their own views. Let's face it: someone who can quote imminent psychological and brain scientists, Mark Twain, Anne Morrow Lindbergh, Anais Nin and J.K.Rowling (to name but a few) merits our respect.

Journaling is a well-known technique used by mental health therapists (such as I was before retirement) and as a spiritual practice. Ann uses her own experience as an educator and essayist to provide useful formats, topics, templates and other "tools of the trade" to guide everyone from the novice to the experienced journal keeper. As a scholar, I was impressed with her Bibliography. (Okay, I read it first to "size up" this author before I read the first chapter). Her work is based on solid research in reputable publications. Still, as I said at the beginning, her conversational style is engaging and accessible to all readers. Quite simply, *The Writing Prescription* is a joy to read even before you pick up your own pen and put words to paper.

Dr Jane Park Cutler, PhD, MSW

In her book, *The Writing RX*, Ann Eichenmuller, has made a convincing case for writing as part of a healthy mental and physical diet. She shares studies that show how writing can lower blood pressure, boost the immune system and make us happier.

Gratitude Journals, memoir stories and poetry allow us to put our experiences – the good, the bad and the ugly, into perspective. Contemplating our inner selves can result in better acceptance of our weaknesses and a higher awareness of our strengths.

Her chapter on poetry writing is particularly enlightening, giving the readers a detailed framework for constructing their beginning poems – from brainstorming for ideas, to choosing a form, to organizing thoughts, to the final edit. The section on "Short Poetic Forms" is the perfect place for novice poets to begin and quickly feel successful in their new craft.

Entire books have been written on the many types of form poetry. Eichenmuller again makes poetry writing approachable by breaking those lists down to their simplest forms – lyric poetry, which is the sharing of personal ideas; and narrative poetry, which tells a story. She also gives the aspiring poet lists of ideas, beginning with something as ordinary as everyday objects…a *photograph; a baby's shoe.* Other idea lists offer conflicting concepts…love/hate; joy/sorrow. The big idea list encourages the writer to tackle topics like birth and death.

Eichenmuller explains that the abstract nature of poetry is one of the reasons researchers believe it can be so effective in helping us to express and understand our emotions. Poetry is food for the soul. A poem about a storm can really be about a storm in the poet's life. The storm becomes a metaphor for that experience and allows us to release emotions too painful to address directly. I especially liked the title of the poetry chapter, Words Like Chocolate, showing within that chapter how words have a taste, a touch, a smell, a feel, like chocolate.

As a poet and also a prose writer, I have often wished for a handbook which encompasses both types of writing. Ann Eichenmuller has written my wish. I can't wait to share this inciteful, beautiful written, carefully researched and constructed book with my critique groups and my students.

Sharon Canfield Dorsey, Vice President Eastern Division
The Poetry Society of Virginia

The professional, helpful advice about why and how to write makes *The Writing Prescription* an inspiring read. Great title, by the way ("prescription" isrelated to "script" and "prescriptive").

Because I also taught writing, the "how" part is familiar to me, but it is appropriate for a lay audience. I like the clear, prescriptive prompts. The suggestions about setting some time to write are more implicit, given as part of the instructions that experimenters gave to participants (write for 20 minutes 3 times a week or something like that).

The "why" part is what I enjoyed the most. The research on the effects of writing on people's physical and mental health is interesting. Some of the studies cited involved a suspiciously low "n," but cumulatively, the evidence persuades me. It helps that at one point the author says something like, "I can feel your skepticism." Part of the reason I am persuaded is that, like the women writers the author talked to about this book, I have personally experienced the healing effects of writing.

My favorite aspect of this book is it tone. I like the way the author addresses her readers. It is respectful, friendly, and other-centered.

She often writes things like, "Remember that thing I mentioned earlier?", "So let's recap," and "If you've been doing the math." I liked noticing that she was thinking of me and all her other readers. Also, little gems of content, like the fact that three participants in a writers group had all experienced the Hindenberg disaster and the author's own experience of writing her way into understanding the most important part of her family's sailing adventure, elevate the book from a dry "how-to" to an entertaining, as well as informative, read.

Beverly Peterson, PhD
Associate Professor of English Emerita, Penn State Fayette

Ann Eichenmuller's book, *The Writing Rx,* is one that I wish I had thought to write. I've always found writing to be a therapeutic activity. Now I have the scientific studies to back up my theory. I agree with the author when she infers that journaling is like praying on paper. She goes many steps further and gives the reader detailed, practical instructions on how to get started with journaling or any other form of writing. *The Writing Rx* is a how-to book for the amateur and the professional, alike. It is a comprehensive writer's manual that I will refer to again and again.

Cindy L. Freeman, Author

The Writing Rx

Using the Healing Power of Writing for a Happier, Healthier Life

Ann Eichenmuller

High Tide Publications, Inc.
Deltaville, Virginia

Copyright © 2018 Ann Eichenmuller

All rights reserved. No part of this publication may be reproduced, distributed or transmitted in any form or by any means, including photocopying, recording, or other electronic or mechanical methods, without the prior written permission of the publisher, except in the case of brief quotations embodied in critical reviews and certain other noncommercial uses permitted by copyright law. For permission requests, write to the publisher, addressed "attention: permissions coordinator," at the address below.

High Tide Publications, Inc.
1000 Bland Point
Deltaville, Virginia 23043
www.hightidepublications.com

First Edition

ISBIN: 978-1-945990-26-7

*To my husband Eric,
for all his love and encouragement*

Contents

1 - Preface	1
2 - Why We Write	7
From Caves to Computers: A Brief History of Writing	9
The Pursuit of Happiness	13
Happiness: Nature or Nurture?	15
3 - The Happiness Prescription	19
Writing Our Way to Happiness?	21
Writing = Positive Thinking	24
Writing = Enhanced Gratitude	26
Writing = A Valued Life	28
Writing = Creativity + Insight = Happiness	31
4 - The Healing Prescription	33
The Drugless Remedy	35
The Power of Paper	38
5 - Journaling: Don't Just Think—Write!	39
A Higher Consciousness	41
Journaling Isn't Just For Kids	43
Journaling: A Menu of Choices	45
What Journaling Can't Do	48
Caution: A Word About Online Journaling	49
How to Journal	50
List Journaling Prompts	52
The Free-Write	53
Free-Writing Topics	55
Diary-style and Reflective Response Journaling	57
Basic Journal Starters #1	59

6 - Letters: Our Naked Truth	61
Letters for Real Life	63
How to Write a Letter	66
Letter-writing Exercises	68
7 - The Memoir:	71
Time Travel Made Easy	71
Going Backwards and Forwards	73
How to Write a Memoir	76
8 - Tasting Words: Poetry	81
Words Like Chocolate	83
How To Write a Poem	86
Poem Starters	89
Short Poetic Forms	92
9 - Opinions, Advice, & the God Perspective	95
Secrets of the Writers' Club	97
The Creative Non-Fiction Smorgasbord	99
How to Write a Creative Non-Fiction Essay	102
The Narrative Essay	105
10 - Resources: Templates, Glossaries & Other Tools of the Trade	107
Glossary of Writing Terms	111
Journaling:	
Free Writing Topics #2	
Basic Journal Starters #2	
Bibliography	
Template A - Basic Mental Map/Brainstorming Web	109
Template B - Storyboard Brainstorming	110
Journaling:	113
Journaling:	114
Free Writing Topics #2	115
Basic Journal Starters #2	116
Bibliography	117
Index	120
About the Author	124

Preface

A story-a true story-can heal as much as medicine can.

Eben Alexander

Proof of Heaven:
A Neurosurgeon's Journey into the Afterlife

Have you looked in the vitamin and supplement aisle recently? It's a little like going down the rabbit hole—one pill to make you larger, one to make you small. With bottles that promise everything from increased libido to sharper thinking, Americans shell out 21 billion dollars a year hoping to buy health and happiness. Unfortunately, there's precious little evidence to prove that these supplements are doing us any good. Meanwhile, just a few aisles away, there is a product you can purchase for under a dollar that a growing body of research suggests can improve your physical and mental health.

It's called a pen.

Turns out your English teacher was right all along. Writing is good for you.

I first became interested in the healing power of writing in an unlikely way. It started with a speech I was scheduled to make at a local women's club luncheon. I pulled up my remarks on the computer that morning and read over them. The introduction was lackluster, and I wasn't sure how to spice it up. After trying a few variations, none of which were quite what I wanted, I decided to put the speech aside and check my email and Facebook. A friend had just posted an interesting quote from a research study that caught my attention. It stated that people who write regularly tended to be both happier and healthier than the general population. Just what I needed to flesh out my introduction! I popped it into my opening remarks without much thought.

My speech lasted about forty-five minutes. Afterwards I did a book signing, expecting to get the usual questions: Is it hard to write a novel? Where did I find the time? How did I create my characters? And, just between us, was the sheriff based on anyone they knew? Instead, I was surprised and a little disconcerted to find that every woman in line wanted to talk to me about the same thing —and it wasn't my novel. Each had latched onto that one quote I had added so casually, and they were eager to share their own stories of how writing had helped them deal with trauma, illness, or loss. No two experiences were alike. One woman was a cancer survivor, one was a widow, another had lost a son–the list went on. What they had in common was their steadfast belief in the healing power of creative self-expression.

I came away intrigued. As a teenager, I remember writing poetry to cope with my mother's cancer; as an educator for more than thirty years, I saw how putting thoughts and experiences in black and white can help adolescents and young adults come to terms with their feelings. As an adult myself, I turned to writing when my husband was injured in an experimental airplane accident. Still, I never consciously thought of writing as anything but a tool for communicating ideas. Now I wondered—were the stories of these women unique, or was there legitimate proof of a healing power in the act of writing?

What I found surprised me.

Research has shown that expressive writing—writing that conveys one's thoughts and feelings—can produce measurable improvements in patients with a range of physical illnesses, from cancer to arthritis to sleep disorders, all without ingesting a single pill. It can lower blood pressure, boost your immune system, and it can even make you happier.

I feel your skepticism. While this book does present some encouraging findings about writing's curative powers, no one is claiming writing as a remedy for everything that ails us. It cannot take the place of a doctor or therapist and is not a substitute for medical treatment. It is not magic.

Think of it as a part of a healthy diet, like whole grains and vegetables. Think of it as mental and emotional weightlifting. Writing: a nutritional supplement and exercise regimen for your body and your soul.

Perhaps the idea of writing makes you uncomfortable. Maybe you are still scarred by your tenth-grade term paper, the one your teacher covered with red ink. Maybe you are afraid that you will misspell words or forget a punctuation mark or—heaven forbid—dangle your participles (whatever that means).

Don't be.

This is writing about you and for you. No one will judge it—in fact, no one even has to see it.

The Writing Prescription isn't a one-size-fits-all regimen. This book is full of choices. How often do you want to write? What kind of writing do you like to do? If daily journaling feels rigid and restrictive to you, you might be more comfortable writing a list once a week. Perhaps you want to write the story of your life to share with your grandchildren or a letter to your brother, owning up to stealing his baseball glove in seventh grade.

Maybe you just want to describe what it feels like to sit on your front porch and breathe.

It's up to you.

If you approach your writing thoughtfully, with a focus on finding meaning, studies show that you will feel better and be happier. My goal is to encourage you to consider creative self-expression as part of a healthy lifestyle and to provide you with the information and tools to get started.

All you have to bring is a pen.

2

Why We Write

I write because I don't know what I think until I read what I say.

Flannery O'Connor

From Caves to Computers: A Brief History of Writing

What does your computer keyboard have in common with a caveman?

More than you might think.

Enter the caves at Chauvet and Lascaux in southern France and you will see an array of images painted in brilliant color across the faces of rock. For decades these drawings of ochre and charcoal were viewed as man's earliest artwork, but recently scientists have developed another theory. Interspersed throughout the realistic depictions of horses and bison are a series of symbols that don't form any identifiable picture. Straight and curved lines, squiggles, ambiguous shapes, they don't seem to have any purpose.

Yet these same symbols appear over and over in many of the more than 200 such archeological sites across France and Spain. Anthropologists now believe they are a kind of shorthand, their creators choosing easily drawn, simple symbols to represent words or phrases. In this way a curved line might have the same meaning as an ornately drawn animal, but it had the advantage of being easily reproduced and recognized by anyone who knew its meaning. If they are correct, these symbols, some dating back 30,000 years, may have been man's first attempt at a written language, and a forerunner to the keys I am tapping now to write this book.

These early cave painters came from a time when existence was a daily struggle and human lives were short. As a species, man had just begun to develop sophisticated tools, and most of his waking hours were occupied with finding food. Why would he waste energy and resources on something as frivolous as writing?

Because writing wasn't frivolous at all.

Think about all of the ways written language serves as a foundation for our society today. Our laws, our system of government, our records, our history, even our spiritual beliefs are all captured in documents and books. What if they didn't exist?

We've all heard the saying "strength in numbers," and that was especially true in the harsh and primitive world of our ancient ancestors. Consider the size of a wooly mammoth—would you want to face one alone? Even if you had a successful hunt, could you stop marauders from stealing your meat? More people in your clan meant better protection, and it also offered a greater chance of successfully raising your young. While these clans began as extended family groups, anthropologists note that at some point the clan would have expanded to included non-family members. They believe this ability to form cooperative social groups was a key ingredient to man's success as a species. But without blood relationships as a unifying factor, how would the clan overcome its natural distrust of outsiders?

Think about what makes a community: common goals, similar beliefs, shared values. How could early man explain these ideas to new members, and how could they pass this culture down to future generations? In the time before written language, the vehicle they used was storytelling, or what is referred to as the oral tradition.

Did you ever complain about cleaning your room or helping in the garden as a child? If so, your parents or grandparents probably told you the fable of the ant and the grasshopper, the one where the grasshopper plays around all summer while the ant busily prepares for winter. When the snow falls, the ant is snug and well-fed, while the grasshopper starves.

Did you ever claim the dog ate your homework? You must have heard the story of boy who cried wolf. If you remember, it doesn't end well for the boy.

Those tales teach the values we want to imprint on our children, like the importance of hard work or of truthfulness. For early societies, oral storytelling was a fundamental advance because important historical information, societal rules and standards could be transmitted from generation to generation through frequently repeated, easily remembered tales.

Mythology, stories used to explain natural phenomena, also developed as a part of the oral tradition. The unknown is frightening; in giving a reason for why an event occurs, man also gave himself a sense of control over the uncontrollable. A volcano eruption could be explained as an angry display of a deity. This gave man the option of trying to appease the deity to stop the destruction. Eventually the eruption would cease naturally, but by linking it to an action he took that corresponded with the time the event ended, man felt empowered.

But of course, the oral tradition has a weakness. It can only be transmitted by word of mouth. Did you ever play the game "Telephone" as a kid? One person whispers a statement or brief story to a neighbor, who in turn repeats it to the next person in a chain. The story goes down the line until the last person, who shares what they heard. The game was entertaining because the final version was usually so different from the original.

That might be funny at a sleepover, but it isn't so amusing if you are trying to pass down the timing of the 50-year flood or your clan's rules about adultery. Misinformation in either case could be…well, use your imagination.

The symbols and pictorial representations found in the French and Spanish caves were some of man's earliest attempts to overcome this weakness and preserve stories in a more permanent form. Scientists have not yet deciphered all of the symbols or determined exactly what they communicate. They cannot say for sure whether the markings are intended to be historical or fictional, but it is clear that they are part of an attempt to tell a story. These easy-to-replicate symbols may have each represented a word or a phrase, and from these crude beginnings alphabets were eventually developed. Linking a symbol to a sound allowed a small number of symbols to be used to create a much greater number of words. The Latin or Roman alphabet used in Western civilizations has only 26 characters, yet an unabridged modern dictionary contains nearly half-a-million words.

This rich vocabulary has allowed the creation of longer, more complex texts, and this is where writing really began to get interesting. Rather than just communicating information or transmitting beliefs for a group, writing was now used individually, to reflect on the human condition and to express personal opinions, imaginings, and dreams. Many of the earliest works of literature are written to make us think not about rules but about the gray areas of morality. Their themes are universal ones—love and hate, truth and dishonesty, trust and betrayal—and not so different from books on *The New York Times* Bestseller List today.

No wonder historians see the development of written language as essential for civilization's "great leap forward." Writing had the staying power oral tradition lacked. Once engraved on stone or written on papyrus, the words maintained their meaning. Unless they were physically destroyed, they could live for centuries, unaltered by time and memory, to be read again and again. It is a power Shakespeare recognized in his eighteenth sonnet, when he compares writing about a woman to giving her immortality:

> *But thy eternal summer shall not fade,*
> *Nor lose possession of that fair thou ow'st,*
> *Nor shall death brag thou wander'st in his shade,*
> *When in eternal lines to time thou grow'st,*
>   *So long as men can breathe, or eyes can see,*
>   *So long lives this, and this gives life to thee.*

All of mankind's greatest and most beautiful ideas—from Galileo's heliocentric planetary system to Thomas Jefferson's Declaration of Independence—gained influence because they were thoughts made real by the act of writing.

It might seem that in our technological age, writing would become obsolete. After all, with apps like Facetime and Skype, we have only to pick up the phone to hear a voice or see a face. We can listen to audio books, watch television, tune into news on the radio. Why then do we spend so much of our time texting and tweeting, blogging and posting? Why were more than 300,000 new titles published in print last year? It seems that whether we do it on a cave wall, a piece of paper, or a computer screen, we gain something by seeing our thoughts in writing.

Some might call it comfort, others release. You might even call it happiness.

The Pursuit of Happiness

There is no question that we have it easier today than our cave-dwelling ancestors. In just the past century, life expectancy for Americans rose 55%, from 49.2 years to 76.5 years. According to the United Nations Human Development Index, our standard of living is among the top 4% of nations in the world. Yet recent polls indicate that 8 in 10 of us experience daily stress, and only 1 in 3 of us is happy.

For a country that lists the pursuit of happiness as one of man's inalienable rights, just behind life and liberty, this is a problem.

Whenever I think about happiness, I think of our neighbor, Henry*. He passed away a few years ago, but one memory sticks with me. I had stopped by to visit, and Henry was propped up on pillows in his easy chair, looking out of the window. He was ninety-five at the time, had recently suffered a heart attack, and his hearing was failing. Yet he never uttered a word of complaint. Instead he drew my attention to the cherry tree outside. "Isn't that the prettiest thing you've ever seen?" he asked. "I can sit here all day and look at that tree."

This was a man who had buried a wife, two sons, and a grandson. It is likely he spent at least a part of each day in pain. Yet against all odds he was still content with his life, still grateful for the beauty around him. He was, in a word, happy.

How can we all be more like Henry?

We know happiness matters to us. The majority of U.S. residents rate personal happiness as very important and report thinking about happiness at least once every day. But for centuries the questions of what exactly happiness is, what it does for us, and how we can get it have been more in the realm of philosophers, poets, and snake oil salesmen than in the purview of the scientific community. Fortunately, that has started to change. Scientists are beginning to realize that happiness is more than just a state of mind. We now have proof that how happy we feel has profound and far-reaching effects on every aspect of our lives.

According to research, happiness has numerous positive byproducts, and its benefit stretch beyond individuals to affect families and communities. On a personal level, happy people have higher odds of marriage and lower odds of divorce, more friends, stronger social support, and richer social interactions. As workers, they exhibit greater creativity, increased productivity, and higher quality of work, thereby earning a higher income. They also tend to be more active and report having higher energy levels than people who demonstrated a more negative outlook.

The benefits of happiness extend to our physical well-being. A recent review of more than 160 studies found "clear and compelling evidence" that happier people have better overall health and live longer than their less happy peers. They are around half as likely to catch a cold virus and have a 50% lower risk of experiencing a cardiovascular event such as a heart attack or stroke. And in case you think happy people are only happy because they are self-centered, the literature suggests the opposite: happy individuals are actually more cooperative, prosocial, charitable, and "other-centered" than their less happy peers.

Basically, happy people are good for themselves, their families, their communities, and society as a whole. So what does that have to with writing?

A lot more than you think.

Happiness: Nature or Nurture?

Knowing we should be happy doesn't make us happy, any more than knowing we should lose weight makes us thinner. Is it possible to increase our levels of happiness, or is it a function of our personalities? In other words, is it nature or nurture? Are people like Henry born happy, or are they made happy?

These are good questions. We've all seen a bit of our parents in ourselves, and we've all been at family gatherings where a relative tells bad jokes loudly or has one too many eggnogs, reminding us of Uncle Bill or Aunt Sue. The saying "The apple doesn't fall far from the tree" exists for a reason. Is our tendency to happiness based in our DNA in the same way as red hair and a snub nose?

Yes and no. Early research in this field did find a genetic component to happiness. For example, identical twins were found to exhibit similar levels of happiness in a variety of situations, while fraternal twins did not. Other studies found that individuals all have an average or base level of happiness. While circumstances such as getting married, giving birth, or losing a job all temporarily increased or decreased people's happiness, afterward they consistently return to their base levels. No event seemed to have the power to permanently alter an individual's basic outlook on life. This supports the idea that a tendency to happiness is inheritable. In other words, some people are just naturally more positive than others.

If that were the end of the story, this would be a pretty short book.

According to Sonja Lyubomirsky, PhD, professor of psychology at UC Riverside and the author of the best-selling book, *The How of Happiness*, we actually have a strong capacity for determining our own happiness. Recent research now suggests that only 50% of a person's happiness is pre-determined by genetics. Scientists call this a set point, similar to the base level found in previous studies. They measured increases and decreases in this level in response to circumstance and found a variation of only about 10%. In other words, a fender bender can cause distress, but it won't automatically cause unhappiness any more than winning the lottery will guarantee happiness.

If you've been doing the math, you've noticed that our natural base level and circumstances only equal 60% of our capacity for happiness. What about the rest?

Research shows that 40% of an individual's happiness is a result of intentional activity. This can be defined as anything we choose to do that can make us feel better or worse and includes an infinite range of behaviors—anything from jogging to drinking a beer, playing video games, and even writing. It turns out that intentional activity is far more important to our happiness levels than the things that happen to us, and nearly as powerful as the emotional traits we inherit.

These findings led researchers to consider a new question—are there activities and behaviors that can specifically target and increase our happiness?

We know physical exercise has an effect on mood. During exercise, the brain releases a chemical called brain-derived neurotrophic factor to protect neurons from the anticipated effects of prolonged physical stress. At the same time, the brain releases endorphins. This chemical numbs pain and facilitates peak performance. Both of these chemicals also induce feelings of well-being. We've all heard of the "runner's high." The happiness inspired by a workout can even be addictive, and studies show that regular exercise can create a biochemical "habit" which provides the same lift for the person exercising as taking a cigarette break does for a smoker.

Spiritual exercise is another intentional activity that has been shown to have emotional benefits. Studies suggest that people who pray or meditate regularly demonstrate qualities like kindness, forgiveness, and trust to a greater degree than the general population and report greater levels of contentment with life.

While habitual physical and spiritual exercise are intentional activities that can increase happiness, there are other activities that have the opposite effect. Drinking alcohol, for example, is something a lot of us do because it temporarily elevates our mood. But alcohol is a depressant, and it works on at least five different neuroreceptors. It has been shown to increase depressive symptoms in individuals prone to depression and can worsen anxiety. A couple of glasses of wine may taste good and may make you feel temporarily relaxed, but they will not make you happy.

All of this brings me back to my neighbor, Henry. He practiced several behaviors that, according to research, could have enhanced his state of contentment. One was daily prayer. Another was observing nature and reflecting on its beauty.

A third was writing.

Henry wrote long letters to his sister several times a week. He told me that he often wrote about memories from childhood or about vacations or holidays their families spent together. He shared details about his daughter and grandsons, the parishioners at his church, and the farm he lived on. When I asked if she wrote as often as he did, he explained that her health did not always allow her to respond. But, he assured me, that didn't matter. "I enjoy the writing, whether I get anything back or not."

We now know Henry was on to something.

3

The Happiness Prescription

If you want to be happy you have to work to make it happen. You can't just wish for it and you can't put it in the hands of other people.

Michael Buckley

The Everafter War

Writing Our Way to Happiness?

When you think of the Sixties, do you conjure up images of Woodstock and Flower Power, Beat poets and Bob Dylan? In a decade devoted to contemplating our inner selves, it is no surprise that writing was viewed as a pathway to emotional wellness. Dr. Ira Progoff, a New York psychologist, popularized the concept of therapeutic writing with his *Intensive Journal Method* workshops. The method consists of a series of writing exercises using loose leaf notebook paper in a three-ring binder, divided into sections meant to help access various areas of the writer's life. The idea caught on and by the 1970's was expanded to a more mainstream audience through Progoff's book, *At a Journal Workshop*, as well as several other best-selling books which repackaged journaling as something for everyone, guaranteed to enhance self-discovery and personal growth.

But like fad diets and other health crazes, journaling outside of a clinical setting lacked empirical evidence for its claims. It wasn't until the 1980's, through the work of Texas researcher Dr. James Pennebaker, that we began to understand expressive writing and just what it could do for us.

Expressive writing is defined as personal writing that expresses and explores the emotions of the writer. It can be an account of an experience in the writer's life, but it can also be writing that answers a question or states an opinion. What makes it expressive is its emphasis on personal feeling rather than events, objects, places, or people.

In his earliest study, Pennebaker placed college students in one of two groups: an experimental expressive writing group and a control group. Participants in the experimental group were asked to write for fifteen minutes on four consecutive days about the most traumatic or upsetting experiences of their lives, while those in the control group wrote about neutral topics like a room or a pair of shoes. No feedback was given on the writing.

Not surprisingly, students who wrote about their deeper feelings showed some distress in the short term, but in the long term they expressed increased feelings of well-being compared to the control group. In other words, writing about the upsetting event actually made them feel happier. There was an added bonus: students who wrote expressively also had significantly fewer visits to the health center and fewer days out of class owing to illness than students in the control group. And these positive effects continued for months beyond the initial experiment.

Why?

Scientists aren't sure. There are several ideas about the mechanism that makes writing work for us. Most researchers agree that writing about a troubling event allows us to structure disorganized thoughts into more cohesive ones, clarifying and validating our reactions and giving us the opportunity to put the experience in perspective. The resolution we get from doing this relieves stress, and it makes us feel better.

Don't reach for your pen yet. No one is recommending that you sit down every day and write about something terrible that happened to you. First, it's not a sustainable exercise because we (hopefully) don't have an endless supply of "most upsetting" experiences. Second, there is nothing to conclusively prove that it was reflecting on the trauma alone that made the experiment a success. Is there something else that occurs when we write, something that makes the physical act of writing itself valuable, regardless of its context? Could writing about good things have the same effect as writing about bad ones?

One avenue of research that might offer some clarification is the study of writing as a tool to develop "happiness habits." Just as weight loss experts study the qualities of thin people to determine how the rest of us can get thinner, scientists are looking at the qualities of happy people to see if there are any treatments or interventions that could be used to make us all happier. We know from research that people with high levels of happiness express joy, contentment, and the perception life is valuable. Their habits—behaviors they repeat regularly—include frequently reflecting on the positive aspects of relationships and events and showing gratitude, and they demonstrate these behaviors far more often than those who are unhappy. Think of happiness as a kind of muscle, like your bicep. If you do enough curls, your bicep muscle will increase in size. Researchers theorized that happiness might also be increased through repeated exercises that mimic habits like positive reflection or expressions of gratefulness. By using writing "interventions" to practice the qualities shared by happy people, and incorporating these interventions in our daily life, is it possible that we could make ourselves happier?

Absolutely.

Writing = Positive Thinking

Positive thoughts don't just happen on their own. They can be created. One method of emphasizing positives is to reflect on a past event that made you feel happy. A 2002 study used this technique by asking college students to relive their happiest day in writing. The study's designers developed a scale for evaluating the positive and negative emotions of words as well as identifying words that signaled greater insight. They then compared the students' use of words with their self-reported level of happiness before and after writing. They found that writing which included higher levels of positive emotion words and increased insight words measurably improved the happiness levels of participants. The more participants focused on being positive as evidenced by their use of positive language, the more likely they were to focus on learning or growing from an experience. The use of greater numbers of positive words directly correlated to how much the better participants felt.

Of course, just like we can't always write about our most upsetting experiences, every day also can't be our happiest day. Most of us don't spend our days hitting home runs or having pina coladas on the beach. The majority of our hours are spent working, eating, sleeping, and doing the mundane but necessary tasks of everyday life. And that's okay. Expressive writing research shows that attitude and perspective about even ordinary events can be changed by the kinds of words we use to write about them—and so can our level of happiness.

Participants in another Pennebaker study were asked to write about their average work day with the instruction to focus on using positive language in their essays. Their responses were analyzed using the same method as the "happiest day" study. Again, those participants who used the highest number of optimistic and insightful words showed corresponding increases in happiness levels. There did not appear to be any correlation between the actual events of the day and the writer's happiness level; the only correlation was the use of positive language. Again, researchers found that those increases were not short-lived; in fact, the increased happiness levels lasted for up to four weeks after the activity was complete.

Writing = Enhanced Gratitude

Another quality common to happy individuals is a sense of gratitude. Defined as the quality of being thankful, we know that demonstrating grateful behavior enhances empathy and represses toxic emotions like anger, jealousy, and frustration. To encourage participants to develop feelings of thankfulness, subjects in a 2003 study were asked to keep gratitude journals once a week, three times a week, or not at all. Participants in the journaling groups were asked to write down up to five things for which they were grateful, with the suggestion that they should try to think beyond inanimate objects like sweaters or cell phones. Not surprisingly, the groups which kept gratitude journals showed increased levels of happiness and well-being, and the more often they wrote, the greater the increase.

Spirituality and writing were paired in another writing intervention study that had subjects pray and write letters to God with an emphasis on giving thanks. Both prayer and letter-writing led to increased insight and higher levels of positive emotions, but it was the letter-writing that had the most significant impact. This supports the theory that the act of writing itself makes an experience more meaningful than merely thinking or speaking aloud.

In another letter-writing study, participants wrote to individuals to express their gratitude for something the person had given them or done for them. These letters were written with the understanding that they would not be mailed. Researchers in this experiment found that the act of writing to express thankfulness produced enhanced feelings of happiness and well-being, and that the exercise was most successful when paired with reflection about past events.

All of this research proves that thankfulness can be enhanced by exercising it. Even if you are a "glass half-empty" kind of person by nature, writing with a focus on gratitude can change your outlook—and that can change your life.

Writing = A Valued Life

One common trait of happy people is the belief that their lives have value and meaning. But it can be hard to feel your life has purpose when you are suffering from an illness and your days are spent in endless rounds of treatment or flat on your back in a hospital bed. Seeing meaning in their lives can be particularly difficult for elderly people, for whom physical limitations, the loss of a driver's license, and the death of friends or loved ones can make aging an isolating experience. Many clinicians in senior and assisted living communities are turning to writing research to develop programs aimed at helping residents reflect on and recognize the value of their lives with the goal of increasing their feelings of happiness.

One such a program is the Goldwater Writing Workshop, which pairs graduate students in creative writing at New York University with long-term care residents at the Coler Goldwater Specialty Hospital & Nursing Facility. Participants attend hour-long poetry workshop sessions led by one of the students. Each session begins with the introduction of a particular poetic form or device, followed by group brainstorming and free writing time. At the end of the session, writers can share their poems.

"Poetry engages both the head and the heart," says Dr. Sondra Brandler, a former professor at the New York University School of Social Work. "It is intellectually stimulating, and it has great therapeutic value in helping people come to terms with the problems of aging."

The combination of a group setting and reflective writing in the poetry workshop has proven highly successful. Residents credit the workshop with keeping their minds "sharp" and making them "feel more a part of a community." They also express pride and pleasure at the products they create, which are published in annually in *The Golden Writers Anthology*.

For those who suffer from a serious illness, regardless of age, expressive writing has been shown to increase a sense of well-being. In a recent Australian study, individuals undergoing cancer treatment for advanced cancers were given the opportunity to participate in a weekly two-hour poetry workshop for eight weeks. The workshop involved reading, writing, and sharing poetry in a group setting, though participants were encouraged to write on their own between meetings. The study found that patients who took part in the poetry group reported significantly lower levels of stress—regardless of the progress of their disease.

"Both writing and psychotherapy provide an opportunity for each individual to create a 'second story' that makes sense of experience, especially when a life-threatening illness has suddenly removed all sense of control," noted the study's authors.

The researchers explained that a response to serious illness tends to follow cognitive steps, and that expressive writing allows patients to move through these to a place of acceptance more effectively. The participant becomes aware of feelings through writing and is then able to place the experience within a broader life context. He or she can then develop a point of view about what is happening, and then achieve a "big picture" understanding that his or her life is about much more than the disease, all facilitated by the poetry workshop.

The memoir is another form of expressive writing that is being used with positive results in treatment centers and senior facilities. Unlike an autobiography, which documents all of the major events of one's life, a memoir is a retelling of a moment or collection of moments and events that were of value to the writer. Facilities that have incorporated memoir-writing classes find that they work on several levels. Socially, the sharing of memories within the class helps participants to connect to each other. Anne Flaxman, a certified instructor with The Center for Journal Therapy, explains that her students are often surprised at how their individual lives have intersected and almost touched. "Three people in one class saw the Hindenburg on its last day," she said. "One saw it fly overhead, one saw smoke in the next field, and one's father was a doctor who was called to the scene."

She also points out that reflecting on the past in writing often gives seniors a new perspective on their lives, seeing them "as jewels that have been polished through time and experience and living."

The completed memoirs are also a legacy that can be passed on to children and grandchildren. For the terminally ill in particular, knowing that someone will remember your story when you are gone can make participants feel more satisfied that their lives had value and purpose.

The poetry workshops and memoir-writing classes have an added benefit—they are inexpensive. In a review of writing research in the journal *The Arts in Psychotherapy*, Dr. Silke Heimes notes that this kind of expressive writing is a "cost-effective therapy that can be applied virtually anywhere and presents a good self-help opportunity." In addition, unlike anti-depressants and other drug therapies, there are no physical risks or complications from therapeutic writing.

Writing = Creativity + Insight = Happiness

Most of the research done on writing for happiness has focused on personal expressive writing, but that does not mean that you cannot get similar benefits from more creative types of writing.

"Creative endeavors are intrinsically rewarding, and you get these little shots of dopamine in the rewards center of the brain," says Shelley Carson, PhD, author and professor at Harvard University, in a recent article in *Psychology Today*.

Creative writing falls into two categories, non-fiction and fiction, though the dividing line between them is not as clear as you might think. Generally, non-fiction is defined as something that is true or actually happened, whereas fiction is a story that is created by the writer. Novels are often set in real places against a backdrop of historical events. The characters, the plot, and even the dialogue may be represented so realistically and in such detail that it is hard to separate them from real life. At the same time, non-fiction can use the same story-telling techniques as fiction. The writer can highlight the emotions of the people he or she is writing about, build suspense or develop romance through his presentation of dialogue, description, and pacing, and communicate a deeper underlying message or theme. For a reader, the only noticeable difference between fiction and creative non-fiction might be where in the library the book is shelved.

Fiction writing—that is, making up stories—taps into many of the same psychological elements as journaling and writing poetry. Author A.M. Holmes points out that there is "an accuracy to fiction that people don't really talk about—an emotional accuracy." The creation of a character is a reflective process, because our characters are made of bits and pieces of ourselves and people we have known. Whether we write mystery or romance or science fiction, our plots will revolve around the same basic conflicts we face to some degree in our own lives and relationships. Ask any author, and they will tell you the same thing —you really can't write creatively without learning something about yourself.

But you don't have to be a novelist to let your artistic side loose in your writing. You can get the same inspiration from writing creative non-fiction. Memoirs, essays, and even how-to books can be both factual and inventive, and depending on how they are approached, writing them can have the same benefits as other types of expressive writing. Research shows us that the power of expressive writing comes from connecting to our emotions, thinking deeply, and reflecting on our lives. Whether you are writing an opinion essay or sharing how to grow a garden, focusing on the feelings you have about your topic, the value and meaning of your knowledge, and how your experiences in an area have helped you to grow are all exercises that have been shown in studies to lead to higher happiness levels.

4

The Healing Prescription

Understanding is the first step to acceptance, and only with acceptance can there be recovery.

J.K. Rowling

Harry Potter and the Goblet of Fire

The Drugless Remedy

In the prologue I talk about the women I met who started me on this quest to understand the healing power of the written word. For many of them, writing wasn't a happiness intervention—it was a survival tool. They suffered from serious health issues, and they believed the act of writing had been not only psychologically therapeutic, it had also been physically therapeutic. They didn't just feel better when they wrote—they got better. Remember that first writing study Pennebaker did in the 1980's? The fact that participants in the expressive writing group had fewer visits to the doctor and missed class less often suggested that writing affected both the mind and the body. Repeated studies over the past thirty years have gone a long way toward proving a tangible connection between writing, psychological benefits, and improved physical health.

In 1999, a team of researchers assessed the effect of expressive writing on the physical condition of patients with asthma and rheumatoid arthritis. They found that writing for twenty minutes on three consecutive days about one or more stressful events had positive, measurable health benefits for up to four months after the initial experiment. Asthma sufferers showed a 13% improvement in lung function, and arthritis sufferers showed a 28% drop in the severity of disease activity. The control group showed no significant improvement.

A study published in 2006 documented the effect of expressive writing on immune function. HIV-infected patients wrote for four days for thirty minutes per day. The intervention group wrote about traumatic and/or emotional experiences, while the control was told to write as unemotionally as possible about their activities of the past twenty-four hours. The CD4 lymphocyte count, a measure of the health of the immune system, showed significant increases in the expressive writing group for up to six months after the writing activity. This suggests that the positive emotional effects of expressive writing can translate into physical changes in the human body.

In a 2013 study, researchers at the University of Auckland in New Zealand had 49 healthy adults, ages 64 to 97, spend 20 minutes a day for three consecutive days writing about upsetting events in their lives (expressive writing) or their daily activities (time management). Two weeks later, the researchers gave participants small puncture wounds on the inside of their upper arms and then monitored their healing. Eleven days after the wound infliction, 80 percent more of those in the expressive writing group had fully healed compared with those in the other group. Again, an exercise originally designed to increase feelings of well-being had the added effect of increasing physical well-being.

This is just a small sample of the work that is being done linking writing to improved health function. In other studies, cancer patients involved in journaling reported benefits such as better physical health, reduced pain, and reduced need to use healthcare services. Individuals with cystic fibrosis showed a significant reduction in hospital-stays over a 3-month period, and poor sleepers reported falling asleep more quickly. Women with chronic pelvic pain reported reductions in pain intensity ratings.

And positive health effects have been shown to occur from a variety of types and genres of writing, not just journaling. In addiction studies, writing poetry has also demonstrated great promise. Women who received treatment for alcohol dependency were placed in two groups, one which engaged in poetry therapy, and one which did not engage in any type of expressive writing. Those who wrote poetry were significantly less likely to relapse than those who did not. Other studies have shown poetry writing to prevent burnout in caregivers of family members suffering from mental or physical illness, and some medical research even suggests that reading poetry aloud can alter an individual's cardiac rhythms.

Writing is also being studied as a therapy for veterans suffering from PTSD. A VA study placed veterans into one of three groups, two writing groups and a control or non-writing group. Those in the two writing groups visited a study website where they received instructions to write for at least 20 minutes on four separate days within a 10-day window. For the expressive writing group, the topic was transitioning from soldier to civilian, and they were asked to write about their deepest thoughts and feelings on this subject. The second writing group wrote factually about the information needs of new veterans.

Results not only confirmed the benefits of expressive writing—they suggested for the first time that even writing not traditionally considered expressive can be helpful, too. Compared with no writing at all, expressive writing was better at reducing PTSD symptoms, including reducing anger, distress, reintegration problems, and physical complaints. But there were fewer differences than expected between the expressive and factual writing groups. The factual writing group also showed fewer PTSD symptoms than the non-writing group, suggesting that writing one's thoughts and opinions, even in an unemotional way, can have a therapeutic effect.

A recent review of several decades of expressive writing research concludes that expressive writing can lead to a wide range of both physical and behavioral improvements, including but not limited to:

- Improved immune system functioning
- Lower blood pressure
- Better lung function
- Better liver function
- Fewer days in the hospital
- Improved mood and feeling of greater well-being
- Reduced depressive symptoms before examinations
- Reduced absenteeism from work
- Improved working memory
- Improved sporting performance

The evidence is there, and with each new study, the body of proof is growing. We may not understand the mechanism that drives it, but we know that writing can at the very least aid in both healing and in coping with the physical and emotional side effects of disease.

The Power of Paper

So let's recap: research shows that writing can make sick people feel better and make healthy people healthier. It can even make you happier. Best of all, writing does not require a prescription and can be done almost anywhere with very little equipment. In fact, research has shown that it really doesn't matter whether you choose a pen or a pencil, a marble composition book or a loose-leaf binder, or even a word processor to do your writing—with one caveat.

There is some scientific evidence showing our minds connect with words on paper differently than words on a screen. Subject of all ages have demonstrated better comprehension and recall of print versus electronic formats. It even appears that print has a greater effect on our emotions.

A recent study at Temple University compared the effectiveness of print and digital ads. They determined that paper ads engaged viewers for more time and caused greater activity in areas of the brain associated with value and desire. They also found that a week after viewing, subjects showed greater emotional response and memory for physical media ads. They believe that the experience of touching paper as well as the physical size and arrangement of words on a page creates a mental map that allows our brains to process information more completely and effectively. We simply don't get as much from pages on screens, which have no real beginning and end and no tactile dimension.

That doesn't mean you can't use a computer. I'm typing the pages for this book on one now. But I strongly recommend that you print out anything you type so that you can hold a hard copy in your hands and read it. The science supports paper, and I want your experience with writing to be as positive and effective as possible.

5

Journaling: Don't Just Think—Write!

I must write it all out, at any cost. Writing is thinking. It is more than living, for it is being conscious of living.

Anne Morrow Lindbergh

A Higher Consciousness

I went into teaching right out of college, with all of the enthusiasm and rose-colored expectations of youth. I would reach every heart and mind! Every student I taught would come to love literature just as much as I did! As a part of my campaign, I declared on day one (to a chorus of groans) that students would be required to keep a journal. Their weekly homework assignment was to write for fifteen minutes on three different nights. My goal was to encourage my students to get comfortable with their own voices and perhaps even incorporate some of the vocabulary we were using in class. Knowing that adolescents often want to write about their private thoughts but might be hesitant to share their innermost feelings with me, I told them they could fold back any pages they did not want me to read. Since the journal was just a completion grade, I told them I would hold folded pages up to the light to be sure they weren't blank, but I promised I would not look at what they wrote.

I still remember my anticipation that first Friday when I collected their journals. It didn't last.

By the time I got through the fourth notebook, I had read five mind-numbing, play-by-play accounts of football practice, three minute-by-minute descriptions of babysitting, and seven complete pages of "I don't know what to write" written on every line. Oh, and a lot of folded pages, which I strongly suspected were filled with nonsensical gibberish.

But Rome wasn't built in a day, and I persevered. I praised anything that showed real emotion, and otherwise my comments were sparing, positive, and empathetic. By Christmas I seldom saw a folded page, and the entries became increasingly detailed. But while I clearly saw my students grow as writers, they began to use the journal in ways

I hadn't foreseen. The writing became more for them than it was for me, a place to make sense of the world around them. Sometimes it was a struggle to understand a divorced parent's bitterness or a friend's betrayal, sometimes a hope expressed, perhaps for the first time, of future dreams. My takeaway was that I grew to appreciate my students as human beings. Theirs was that they grew to understand and appreciate themselves. Along the way, their writing improved, though I don't know that anyone ever voluntarily used a vocabulary word.

At the end of the year, when I surveyed students anonymously about what they felt was most valuable in my class, it wasn't acting out plays or group projects or grammar games that got the highest rating—it was, overwhelmingly, the journal.

I continued to assign journals for more than three decades, to thirteen-year-old middle schoolers, high school seniors, and even college sophomores. Because I was dealing primarily with adolescents and young adults, there were times when the journals became more than an exercise in introspection—they became a cry for help. Bullying, harassment, physical and sexual abuse, and neglect all found their way onto those pages, and it broke my heart. At the same time, I am grateful that the journal gave those students a safe place to express their pain, because it allowed us to provide the assistance they needed to escape or overcome difficult situations.

Journaling Isn't Just For Kids

It is easy to understand why journaling works so well with young people. After all, they are undergoing rapid physical, emotional, and even life changes. No wonder they need a tool to organize and examine their thoughts. But once we grow up and get out in the real world, do we really need to write down how we feel?

The view that life after twenty-five or thirty is a stable drive down a well-travelled road is simply not true in the twenty-first century. About 40% of us will divorce at least once, and most of us will change jobs ten or more times in the course of our working lives. We tend to move an average of eleven times and nearly half of us don't have a 401K or a pension. Add to that an increasing number of us who care for elderly parents and have grown children returning home, and adolescence starts to look like the calm before the storm.

Take Candace*. She began keeping a journal in her thirties, when she discovered her husband was having an affair. She wrote in it throughout their divorce and continued to write during her years as a single mother. There was no formula to her writing; at times emotional, at times mundane, it gave her an outlet for thoughts and feelings she could not share with her young children. In it she catalogued other relationships, worked through her anger, and years later wrote about her reconciliation with her ex-husband. Now retired and a grandmother, Candace recently re-read all of her journals and then put them through the shredder.

"They fulfilled their purpose," she said, crediting the writing with helping her to cope with the changes in her life. "I wouldn't want anyone else to read them. I wrote them for me."

A journal is often an on-again, off-again activity for adults. In my own life, months can go by without feeling a need to write expressively, and then a new experience, a family conflict, or a traumatic event suddenly has me sitting at my desk again, putting pen to paper for days or weeks at a time. Journaling for a specific time period or purpose is not unusual. For Susan*, a cancer survivor, writing during the year she underwent treatment helped her to deal with her disease. She wrote every day during her chemotherapy and radiation, and she found it eased the pain and fear and allowed her to cope with the roller coaster emotions that accompanied the treatment.

"Putting it down on paper validated what was happening to me," she explained. "Once I could see it in black and white, it just seemed easier to face."

Many people I have met have made the same observation. Something about the act of writing gives you a sense of power over the subject. We are made anxious by those things we cannot see, define, or understand. Perhaps writing's magic is that it empowers us to give a name to our pain—and to our joy as well. Journaling encourages us to look inside ourselves, and also to examine and appreciate our relationships with others. And that works for all of us, regardless of age.

Journaling: A Menu of Choices

The List

One form of journaling that almost everyone can find accessible is the list. I tried journaling when I had my first child and simply couldn't get a coherent thought together, so instead of trying to write out a paragraph of sentences, I wrote a numbered list. I used this technique to help clarify my feelings and my concerns about parenting. I remember writing "The Five Pieces of Advice Most Often Given by Total Strangers" and "Five Things I Wish Everyone Understood About Being a New Mom." Listing gave me a fresh perspective on how great a change motherhood made in my life.

I recently turned to listing again when I took early retirement at 53. I woke one winter morning and realized I was utterly depressed despite having planned for this most of my life. I wrote "Ten Things No One Tells You About Retirement" and in doing so I realized what was bothering me most. I prioritized the list into things I could change, like needing some kind of schedule in my life, and then I worked on finding solutions.

Free-Writing

Free-writing is just what it sounds like—writing without structure or form, a kind of pouring out of thoughts and emotions on paper. Suppose you are thinking about your mother. What details come to mind? Are you struck by a perfume she wears, a memory of her hand on your forehead when you were sick, the way you felt when she held you in her lap? Jot these images down as they pop into your mind. Don't worry about using capital letters or punctuation or about whether your thoughts make sense.

For me, free-writing is a way of getting down to the heart of a topic. When I was teaching, I would often assign free-writing to my students, and I always sat at a desk in the room and wrote alongside them. Once I had them free-write on their favorite place. I chose my garden, which I love, but when I re-read my "written brainstorm" I noticed I had a pattern of negative words and phrases describing weeds and weather and insects that outweighed the positive images. The overall impression of the writing was frustration, and I realized I wasn't just talking about my garden but about an underlying sense of loss of control in my life.

The Diary

Most journals begin as chronicles of our daily lives. We use them to comment on events and relationships as they happen, and sometimes to reflect on how our present is related to our past. These kinds of entries are written in paragraph form from our own perspective. They can be helpful when we are faced with a difficult period in our lives because recording what is happening can help us to better analyze and understand it. Reading over these kinds of entries days, weeks, or months later can give us perspective on the past and help us to recognize personal growth.

Reflective Response

Often in response to a prompt, these paragraph-style journal entries guide us to focus on specific topics and to think more deeply about how we respond to events and to imagined possibilities. This is the type of expressive writing most commonly used in writing research, and study author Dr. James Pennebaker has some suggestions to make the experience more meaningful. He recommends choosing a time and place where you're unlikely to be interrupted and writing continuously about something that's concerning you for at least 15 minutes on four consecutive days.

"It can be related to something you're dreaming, thinking or worrying about a lot, an issue or memory that's affecting your life in an unhealthy way, or a subject you've been avoiding for days, weeks or years," Pennebaker says.

We can also learn more about ourselves by projecting into the future (Where do you hope to see yourself in 5, 10, or 20 years?) or reminiscing about the past, or even fantasizing about what we would do if we were freed from the constraints of normal life (Suppose you never had to pay another bill. What would you do?)

While many of the students I've worked with start off writing diary entries, as they become more comfortable thinking creatively they always shift to reflective response or free-writing for at least some of their journaling. We know from the research that deeper, more thoughtful writing resulted in the greatest increase in feelings of well-being, so it is no surprise that these types of journaling are often seen by students as more valuable and personally rewarding.

What Journaling Can't Do

As much as I believe journaling can be beneficial, we need to be clear about what journaling can't do. It is unlikely that you will instantly "feel better." Stirring negative emotions can lead initially to feeling upset or unhappy, though studies show that these reactions are usually short-lived. Psychologists also note that you are probably not going to achieve an emotional catharsis, a complete release from negative emotions, from journaling alone. If you are particularly troubled by a memory, consider using the journal as a part of a conversation with a counselor or therapist.

"You need focused thought as well as emotions," cautions Dr. Susan Lutgendorf of the University of Iowa. "An individual needs to find meaning in a traumatic memory, as well as to feel the related emotions, to reap positive benefits from the writing exercise."

Caution: A Word About Online Journaling

I have had several people ask me if blogging or posting on Facebook or other social media sites can have the same therapeutic effect as journaling. Common sense says no. When we write something to post, even though we type out our thoughts in private, we are still aware that they will be read by a multitude of others. We may find ourselves writing for our audience as opposed to writing for ourselves. If you are concerned about whether your friends will "like" your post or what kind of comments you will get in response, how honest and introspective can you be? And posts on social media have an infinite lifespan. Just because you delete something from your feed, it doesn't mean it wasn't copied and re-posted or shared a thousand times over. While you may grow and change, the words you posted online will remain the same, and they could very well come back to haunt you at a family dinner or in a job interview.

If your goal in writing is improved physical and emotional well-being, you may also want to consider a recent Ohio State University study. It found that depressive scores increased for participants who spent more time on social media sites like Facebook, Instagram, Twitter, and YouTube. These findings are echoed in at least a half-dozen other studies conducted in just the past five years. Social media may be a great way to keep up with old friends or see photos of your grandkids, but don't expect journaling online to make you a happier person.

How to Journal

Journaling Lite: The List

Directions:

Write a list of items in response to a chosen prompt.

- Responses should be a sentence or more in length and should describe rather than name.
- Responses should focus on personal feelings and should seek to understand why you feel the way you do.

After Writing:

When you have finished your list, read over your responses. Ask yourself questions like "Does anything I've written stand out to me?" and "What does my writing tell me about myself?"

Example A:

List five things you are grateful for this week.

Sample responses:

- I am grateful that my husband comes up behind me when I am cooking and kisses me on the neck because it makes me feel loved.
- I am grateful for the irises coming up in my front flower bed. They come back for me every spring, like an old friend, and I feel the kind of warmth you feel for pets or children, because I put them there. I planted them.

Notice that I didn't just list "my husband's kisses" or "irises." Instead, I tried to look more deeply into why I was grateful. By doing so, I focused on positive feelings about my husband and myself.

Example B:

List five things you wish someone had told you about this stage of your life. Here are some sample responses:

- You're never going to get more than two hours of sleep at a time.
- You're going to feel just as hormonally unhinged as you did at thirteen.
- You are going to be amazed at some of the things that come out of your own mouth.
- If you are a woman with hot flashes, layers are your new best friend.

These responses are part of a list about my experience of menopause. While I am venting about the changes in my body that make me crazy, by writing about them I am also normalizing them. The hint of humor in the writing shows I am beginning to accept these symptoms as a rite of passage for this stage of my life.

Sometimes you may know exactly what you want to write about and you can create your own list prompt. If not, ask yourself if you are anticipating anything, if anything is bothering you, or if there are aspects of your life that you think you need to change. You can use that information to form a list prompt. If you're still drawing a blank, use the topic suggestions for list journaling on the next page or in the resources section of Chapter 10 to get you started.

List Journaling Prompts

1. List five things you wish someone had told you about this stage of your life.
2. Give five examples of a friend, relative, or stranger's kindness.
3. List three things you saw or did this week that made you feel peaceful.
4. List five things you love.
5. List five places you've been that you really enjoyed.
6. List three things you've done that you never thought you could or would do.
7. List your four favorite books.
8. Think of three goals you'd like to accomplish next week that no one else can see.
9. List the five people in your life you admire most.
10. List five things that you are grateful for.
11. Name three personal goals you'd like to accomplish in the next five years.
12. List your three favorite vacations from your childhood.
13. List your four favorite toys growing up.
14. Name the five most beautiful sights you have ever seen.
15. List your three favorite songs.

The Free-Write

Directions:

1. Think of a person, place, object, or emotion, either from the list or on your own.
2. Close your eyes and visualize the word you chose.
    - What colors do you see?
    - Think of its shape, its edges, its curves.
    - Imagine how it looks in the sun, in the rain, or in moonlight.
    - Does it remind you of anything else?
3. Engage your other senses.
    - Touch it with your lips, the bare skin of your cheek, your toes.
        - Is it warm or cool?
        - Run some bit of it between your fingers, feel the texture. What else feels like this?
    - Breathe it in. What do you smell? How does it make you feel?
    - Taste it. Is it salty, sweet, bitter, sharp?
    - Be still and listen. What sounds do you hear?
4. Open your eyes. For five to ten minutes, write down everything you saw, touched, tasted, smelled, and heard.

After writing:

Read over your list. What one word best describes the overall mood or feeling of what you have written? Add that as either the title or last line of your free-writing entry.

Example:

Myself at 15

- Tall gangly awkward legs too long
- Thick hair dark curls unrestrained like vines reaching grabbing trying to escape uncontrolled
- Corduroy pants rough silky shirt slipping pulling tight buttons gaping revealing skin
- Hands soft pink young plump lips slightly swollen
- Perfume like baby powder or donuts, sweet
- Unrestrained innocence

Note that there is no attempt to organize thoughts into sentences or use punctuation. The first six lines are part of the initial free-write, while the last line is a reflection. The images presented by the writer are in some respects opposites; words like gangly and awkward, soft, and baby powder imply innocence, while images like silky shirt…pulling tight…revealing skin and lips slightly swollen suggest a latent and potent sexuality. The two words at the end refer to these opposites and show that I am thinking about the conflict between being a child and becoming a woman that I experienced as an adolescent.

Free-Writing Topics

Places:

- The beach on a hot day in August
- Your grandmother's kitchen on Thanksgiving
- An open field with an approaching thunderstorm
- The garden in winter
- A crowded city street at twilight
- The car on a long drive

Objects

- A baby's shoe
- Broken glass
- A baseball glove
- A dog collar
- A tube of lipstick
- A quilt

People

- Your spouse/significant other
- Your mother
- Your father
- Your employer
- Your elementary school teacher
- Your best friend

Animals

- An eagle flying
- A cat stalking prey
- Your dog when you come home
- A squirrel
- A mouse in your pantry
- A deer

Diary-style and Reflective Response Journaling

Description:

Write in response to a chosen prompt or as a summary and reflection of your experiences that day. You can write thoughts as they come to you—don't worry about using complete sentences or correct punctuation.

- If you do diary-type entries, don't just report events—reflect on your thoughts and feelings about them.
- Be as detailed and descriptive as possible.

Reflection:

When you have finished writing, read over your journal entry. For diary-style entries, ask yourself questions like "What can I learn about myself from today?" and "Is there anything under my control that I would change about today if I could?"

For other types of entries, think about what stands out or surprises you in what you've written, and what insight it can give you about yourself.

Examples:

Diary-style Entry

I had lunch with the regional manager today. He stopped by my desk and asked me to go. I'm not sure why. It's not like we're friends. He's an all right guy, but I don't really know him. I thought it might be about Ed, like he might want some dirt, but he never brought it up. We talked about fishing and the kids, and he did ask me if I ever thought about leaving the department, maybe transferring to corporate. I don't know if it was a hint or what, but I said I was open to change. That's a lie, because I know we can't move right now with Ellen's job.

Reflective Response

If I knew I was going to live forever, I don't know what I'd do. It's kind of like when you're a kid and it's summer vacation. You know you've got two months so you put stuff off and sometimes you sleep late or don't do anything but watch T.V. I'd be kind of afraid that I'd waste my time because it wouldn't have any meaning. I wouldn't appreciate it.

Basic Journal Starters #1

1. If you knew you could not fail, what is one thing you would like to try?
2. What qualities are most important in a friend?
3. If dogs (or cats) could talk, what would yours say to you?
4. If you could have a conversation with anyone, living or dead, who would it be? What would you talk about?
5. If money were no object, what one thing would you like to do?
6. If you could have three wishes, what would they be? How do you think they would work out for you?
7. If you knew you would live forever, how would that change what you did tomorrow?
8. How would your best friend describe you?
9. If you could trade places with anyone now or in the past, would you? If so, who would it be? If not, why?
10. If you could become an expert in anything, what would it be?
11. Describe your idea of the perfect day.
12. What is your favorite holiday memory?
13. What was the best part about being a kid?
14. How did you see your mother/father/sister/brother when you were a child? How do you see them now?
15. If you could address the nation, what would you tell them?

6

Letters: Our Naked Truth

In a man's letters you know, Madam, his soul lies naked, his letters are only the mirror of his breast, whatever passes within him is shown undisguised in its natural process. Nothing is inverted, nothing distorted, you see systems in their elements, you discover actions in their motives.

Samuel Johnson

Letters for Real Life

Purposefully addressing your thoughts to someone adds an additional dimension to expressive writing. You intentionally consider the intended receiver, and this awareness influence not only what you write but how you write it. This is true even if the letter cannot or will not be sent.

One purpose of expressive letter writing is to deal with something unfinished in your life. For this reason it is sometimes called transactional writing, meaning that the letter itself is a transaction in which you as the writer hope to gain something, like resolution of a past experience or relationship.

Another goal of expressive letter writing is the development of empathy. As a part of addressing our ideas to someone else, we are naturally encouraged to see situations through their eyes and to try to understand events from their perspective. Empathy doesn't mean agreement—you can disapprove of another's decisions or actions but still have an awareness and appreciation for why they behaved as they did.

Letter-writing leads to self-reflection. Because we are addressing another, we choose our words more carefully, and we aim to be more precise. This provokes an honesty we might not always achieve in journaling.

While journals are usually more free-wheeling and unstructured, letter writing follows an established format. It has a greeting and a closing. It attempts to follow conventions of grammar, spelling, and punctuation. It is clearly organized because its purpose is to communicate rather than simply explore thoughts and feelings. While it may feel more restrictive, this structure is also one of letter-writing's strengths. It provides an avenue to consider and clarify your feelings, opinions, beliefs, and judgements while being more conscious of how they affect you and your relationships with others.

Gayle*

I met Gayle many years after a particularly ugly divorce. She and her husband had been together for twenty-seven years and had two adult children when he had suddenly decided he no longer wanted to be married. In her mid-fifties at the time, she was alone and without direction—and she was bitterly angry. On the surface Gayle picked up the pieces of her life, but internally she was incapable of moving past the betrayal. She sought out a counselor, who suggested she write a letter to her ex-husband.

"I needed a chance to get out all of the things I wanted to tell him and didn't," she says.

But something happened when she wrote the letter. She felt less like a victim. Putting her grievances on paper validated them, but they also let her focus for the first time on his perspective, why he behaved as he did, and how she might have contributed to the dissolution of their marriage. It did not result in immediate forgiveness, but for Gayle, it was the first step in letting go and moving on with her life.

Peter*

A man in his fifties, Peter had recently lost a brother to kidney disease. Although they had not quarreled, he and Robert had not been close. Peter felt that was owing at least in part to an incident that had happened fifteen years earlier. Robert had become seriously ill and been diagnosed with total kidney failure. He was placed on dialysis, but he desperately needed a new kidney. Peter's mother had called, asking him to undergo the necessary tests to see if he was a compatible donor. If so, his mother would pay to fly Peter to San Francisco so he could donate a kidney to his brother.

At the time of the call, Peter had three small children. His wife was a teacher, and they needed both of their incomes to stay afloat. In addition, he had been dealing with health issues himself. Though it made him feel guilty, he did not want to jeopardize his own family to save his brother's life. He put off the testing, trying to get up the courage to tell his mother and brother how he felt. In the meantime, his brother's condition worsened. Fortunately, another donor was found, and Peter was never forced into a decision, but he knew his brother had sensed his hesitancy. Though neither of them ever brought it up, he felt it had subtly poisoned their relationship. Now that Robert was dead, the guilt for his part in their estrangement was eating away at him.

One day over lunch he told the story to a friend. She suggested that he write a letter to his brother, explaining his feelings and asking forgiveness for not being honest sooner.

"I cried when I was finished," Peter says. "I had this feeling that Robert was reading it while I wrote it, and he wanted me to know he understood."

How to Write a Letter

General Letter-Writing Directions:

Before Writing

1. Determine Your Audience

For Gayle and Peter, the audience for the letters was already clear. Each had "unfinished business" with someone in his/her past. But your intended audience may not always be another individual. Sometimes the person you need to speak to most is yourself.

We all blame ourselves at some point for events that have happened in our lives. Suppose we had the power to go back and talk to our younger selves, to forgive ourselves for our mistakes? Or suppose we want to talk to our future selves to discuss a decision we are facing? Writing to a younger or older version of you provides an opportunity to gain a new understanding of yourself.

Many of us share a belief in a higher power, even though we not agree on religious practices or conventions. If you spend time in prayer, consider writing a letter to God as well. How often do we take the time to truly thank God for the people and situations in our lives? The structure and organization of this type of expressive writing encourages more serious and thoughtful communication than a hastily whispered grace or bedtime blessing and can have a powerful effect on the writer.

2. Let your choice of recipient drive the type of letter you write.

I have provided some basic categories of letters with accompanying exercises. Read over them and decide which best fits your intended audience and follow the writing instructions.

After Writing

1. Read over your letter carefully. Is there anything that doesn't ring true? Is there something more you need to say? If so, go back and edit. Letters dealing with traumatic events may take several drafts before you feel satisfied that you have written everything you wanted.

2. Once complete, you will need to decide what to do with this tangible evidence of your feelings. Most expressive letters are meant only for us. If you are considering sending any letter from these exercises, stop and think about the possible consequences. Is the letter likely to have a positive effect on the reader? Is it possible that feelings you've expressed might cause emotional harm to the recipient or anyone else they share the letter with? If you still feel someone can benefit from the letter, I recommend putting it in a drawer, out of sight, for a month or more. This will give you emotional distance from the writing experience and guarantee a more reasoned judgement.

3. If you decide your letter should not be sent, you can do what many writers choose to do—shred or burn your letter. If you have used the exercise as a search for meaning, the act of writing will have led to a shift in perspective. Destroying the letter is a way of symbolizing that the past no longer has a hold over you. Think of it as a celebration, a rite of passage, or one more check off the bucket list—your way of saying "I choose happiness."

Letter-writing Exercises

The Gratitude Letter

Think of someone you care about deeply. This can be a relative, friend, God, or even a younger version of yourself. Write a letter thanking him or her for a gift or gifts you have been given. It could be something they gave you, something they taught with you, or something they did that inspired you or made you happy. Describe the context in which gift or gifts were given, how you felt when you received them, and the impact they had or continue to have on your life. As you write, think about the emotions you want to convey and the way you hope your reader will feel as he or she reads the letter.

The Letter of Understanding

Think of someone who has gone or is going through a challenging or difficult experience. This can be yourself, someone you know well, or someone you barely know at all. You may disapprove of how they are handling things or even feel that they are partially responsible for the circumstances in which they find themselves. Write a letter letting them know you feel empathy for their situation, focusing on communicating caring, acceptance, and encouragement. While writing, try to imagine yourself in this person's situation. How would you feel? What would you need from other people? What words would you most like to hear? You may share similar experiences of your own and how you grew or changed as a result but avoid preaching or giving advice.

The Unfinished Business Letter

If you have some distressing event in your past that still bothers you, write a letter to the other person involved about what happened. Before you write, ask yourself what you would need to be able to forgive this person. As you describe the event, try not to focus on how "wrong" or cruel the other person was but instead on why they acted the way that they did. When you describe how you felt, go beyond surface reactions and concentrate on your deepest feelings. What actually hurt you the most? Was it their words and actions, or the destruction of some expectation you had about your relationship with them? Examine any experiences in both of your pasts which might have influenced the outcome. Consider whether the other person might feel differently now about the things they said or did. Consider whether you feel differently about your own actions. Finally, think about how your own life can change if you can forgive.

The I'm Sorry Letter

Think about something you have done that might have hurt someone else. This could be someone close to you, God, or even yourself. Write a letter describing the incident and asking to be forgiven. As you write, think about circumstances that might have led up to the event, how you behaved, and how you might have handled things differently. Try to understand how your actions affected the reader, and how they also affected you. Consider whether there is anything you can still do to make amends.

The Letter to the Future

Write a letter to yourself or someone you care about as if it will be read at some time months or years from now. Some examples are a letter to a grandchild to be opened on their graduation or wedding day, a letter to a spouse at the start of retirement, a letter to yourself when you have a daughter or son the age you are now. In your letter, share your appreciation for their role in your life. Impart any bits of wisdom you feel will enrich their lives. Describe your hopes for the future. Focus on what your reader needs or wants at this point in his or her life, and offer your support and encouragement.

What Letter Writing Won't Do

- You cannot change the past. Do not write your letter expecting that it will alter the opinions or feelings of anyone else. The purpose of letter-writing is to understand your own role in events and/or to bring about a shift in your own perspective.

- Do not expect overnight results. Put your letter aside and come back to it in a few days or a week and see if you feel any differently when you re-read it.

- Do not use letter-writing on your own to address seriously traumatic events in your life. Instead, seek out a trained therapist who can walk you through some of the more destructive emotions involved in dealing with those types of memories.

7

The Memoir:

Time Travel Made Easy

We write to taste life twice, in the moment and in retrospect.

Anaïs Nin

Going Backwards and Forwards

Noted author William Zinsser once wrote, "One of the saddest sentences I know is 'I wish I had asked my mother about that.' " In an essay on memoirs, he points out that it isn't until we begin to feel "the first twinges of advancing age" that we suddenly wish we knew more about family history. Unfortunately, by the time we think to ask, it is often too late. I wish I had asked my grandmother what it was like to come of age during the Great Depression, or what it was like when my grandfather went off to fight in World War II. I never did, and now I can only guess at what she would have said.

Research has shown us that writing and sharing our memoirs can help us come to terms with elements in our past.

"We think the process of creating a coherent story out of disorganized emotional memories facilitates self-distancing because this process requires people to adopt other people's perspectives and focus on broader contexts," explains Jiyoung Park, an assistant professor of psychological and brain sciences at the University of Massachusetts–Amherst, and author of a pair of studies published in the April 2016 journal *Emotion*.

But for many of us, the purpose of the memoir is not solely to "feel better" about the past. In most cases, memoirs are written to be shared. The reason we record bits of our past is that we believe we owe it to our families to leave some trace of ourselves behind. We write memoirs to preserve our voices, the essence of who we are, our memories in writing becoming a priceless gift we can give to our loved ones.

If you are not just writing for yourself, the idea of your children or grandchildren reading what you wrote may make your uncomfortable. After all, you'll say, I'm no writer. My memoir isn't going to sound smooth and polished like something they'd read in a book.

And it shouldn't. You are a character, a narrator, telling your own story. Your family wants to hear your voice, the cadence of your speech, the words you always use, or the memoir will not be authentic.

Perhaps you're worried that something you write will offend a family member. That is a possibility. But for a memoir to be real, it must be truthful. That doesn't mean you should write to prove someone wrong or exact revenge. Remember that writing can only benefit us if we use it to seek understanding. If you write about events with integrity, honesty, and a focus on learning from the experience, the people who care for you should respect the writing even if they do not like what you have to say. A reader will know if you are being dishonest, and in the end shading the truth may cause more discord than the truth itself.

Even if you feel comfortable writing about your life, it is easy to feel overwhelmed with the concept of writing a memoir. Where do you begin? How do you tell the story of your whole life?

You don't. You're not writing an exhaustive autobiography. You're not attempting to chronicle your existence from your first breath to the present. Remember the old joke about how to eat an elephant? The answer was "One bite at a time." A memoir is written in small bites. It is a retelling of a single event or a series of events around a theme. Your memoir can be an essay of a few pages or a collection of a dozen or two dozen such essays, stretching to hundreds of pages. Your memoir can be limited to a very short period in your life—say a three-week vacation to Alaska or the time you tried to start a garage band—or it can cover a much longer time span while staying focused on small, singular incidents within that frame.

My first experience with memoir-writing came a few years ago when my editor at a sailing magazine asked me to write an essay about our family's sail to the Bahamas. Because I was writing for a consumer publication, I didn't have the luxury of choosing a length. I was given 5 pages, including photographs, or about 2000 words. I didn't see how I could condense 2 ½ months and so many memories into such a small space, but it was the first feature the magazine had offered me, and I was afraid to say no. Plus, they were offering three times what I was currently being paid for my stories.

I took the assignment and then struggled for days to come up with an outline or plan. I finally came up with the idea of doing a brainstorming web of all the most vivid memories from the trip. When I was finished, I started grouping the memories by what they had in common. In doing so, I had an epiphany—I realized that I had started the journey with one desire and ended with another. What mattered to me, what I had really wanted when we were planning the trip, was an adventure, but what mattered most to me by the end was the closeness I felt to my husband and children. I distinctly remember wanting to grab the wheel and turn the bow out to sea when we made the final turn toward home, because I knew that we would never again feel the bond between us in the same way. All of the exhilaration and terror of the trip—the storms, running aground, snorkeling in crystal clear waters, catching fish offshore—was backdrop for the real story, which was how we changed as a family by living on a 33 ft. sailboat together.

I cried while I was writing that piece, and my husband had tears in his eyes when he read it. Even my editor got a little choked up. That piece was successful because I found the heart of the experience, the true meaning of it, and now I have record of that time as I saw it and felt it, preserved for posterity.

There are many ways to approach writing a memoir. The exercises that follow are merely a starting point based on my own experience, a place to begin but certainly not a place you need to end.

How to Write a Memoir

The Single Event Memoir

Directions:

1. Choose a topic below.

Personal Memoir

I remember a time when I...
- wanted something badly
- was humiliated or embarrassed
- did something without meaning to
- did something I still don't understand
- was proud of myself
- did something I regret
- knew I was in trouble
- tried to walk away but couldn't
- did something I had dreamed of doing
- got something I wished for
- learned something unexpected about someone I loved
- took the blame for something I didn't do

Historical Memoir

Fill in the sentence below with a historic event that happened during your lifetime and had an impact on your life.

I remember when _____

_____

2. Write a single phrase or sentence naming the memory you chose in a circle in the middle of a sheet of paper. Use Template A, the Basic Brainstorming Map, as a model.

3. For fifteen minutes, write down every detail you can remember about the experience in the circles around the center. Think about who was with you, when and where the incident took place, what you said or did, what others said or did, and how you felt before, during, and after the incident.

4. Look for connections between what you've written. Draw lines between connecting ideas and write a few words on the line explaining the connection.

5. Now go back over the pieces of information you've written one at a time. Close your eyes and try to create a mental image of each. Imagine you are there, in that place and time. What are your senses experiencing? What can you see, hear, taste, smell, and touch? What is the color and tone and texture of the memory? Open your eyes and add these details in spokes around the original piece of information.

6. Read over your brainstorming as a whole. What did you want in the beginning of the event? Did what you want change in the end? Can one word describe the overall emotion you felt, or did your emotions change during the course of the event? How do you feel about the event now?

- Based on what you have written, why was this event important to you—what did you gain or lose by living it?

- Imagine someone has asked you to explain what you have written. For five minutes, begin to tell the story of the event aloud.

- Now write your memory of the event. Use the same kind of language you used when you were speaking. Stay as close to the truth of your memory as possible. Set a goal of two to three pages.

After Writing

Read over what you have written. Add any details you might have just remembered. Ask yourself:

- What have I learned from writing this?
- What do I want someone reading it to learn about me?
- Does the writing accomplish this goal?

If the answer to the last question is yes, move on to editing. If not, think about what you could add or delete to make your central idea more evident to your reader.

Revise and Edit

Use the checklist below to review your memoir. Rewrite until you are satisfied that you have completed each item to the best of your ability.

___ Does my story have a clear beginning, middle, and end?

___ Is it organized in a way that will make sense to my reader?

___ Have I stayed faithful to the truth as I remember it?

___ Have I used words and images that will paint a picture in the mind of my reader?

If you plan to share your memoir with others, you may want to ask a friend or relative to read over your memoir for errors in spelling or punctuation that could interfere with understanding.

The Multiple Event Memoir

Directions

1. Choose a time period in your life that has special significance to you. Examples could be a summer spent with your grandparents, basic training for the military, your first year of college, etc.

2. Write a single phrase or sentence naming the time period/longer event you chose in a square at the top or far end of a storyboard diagram. Use Template B Storyboard Brainstorming as a model.

3. Fill in information about who was a part of the time period. Add details to describe each person.

4. Think about 3-5 incidents or events that occurred during that time period. Write a phrase that identifies each in chronological order in the boxes for beginning, continued, and end.

5. For each incident, write a few words giving details about what happened and how you or others felt. Add as many boxes as you need.

6. Look over your brainstorming. Is there a single emotion, lesson, or theme common to all or most of the incidents? Can you identify changes in your emotion or attitude from the first incident to the last?

7. Based on what you have written, why was this time period important to you—what did you gain or lose by living it?

8. Imagine someone has asked you about the time period you chose. Talk aloud about this time period for 5 minutes.

9. Now write about the time period you've chosen. Use the same kind of language you used when you were speaking. Stay as close to the truth of your memory as possible. Tell about the events in chorological order, setting a goal of one-half to one page per individual event.

Use the After-Writing checklist on page 78 to help you revise and edit your writing.

8

Tasting Words: Poetry

In its compressed use of language to express universal truths, in its bursts of insight, poetry provides glimpses of beauty that can put the challenges of life in perspective.

Alan Lenhoff

Words Like Chocolate

I have a confession to make—though I have written poetry since I was four or five years old, I never really liked it. The poetry that appeared in my elementary and middle school texts was usually very structured, its language dense, its meaning (at least to me) incomprehensible. It wasn't until college that I came to view poetry as alive and accessible, thanks in part to the efforts of my creative writing professor. He emphasized there was far more to words than their dictionary definitions; each word had a taste, a touch, a smell, a feel, born of its connotative meaning. Words can evoke emotions both universal and uniquely individual in the minds of readers. Like chocolate.

Understanding ourselves means understanding how and why we react to words in the way we do. Long before research supported the use of journaling and poetry to improve our physical and mental health, this professor insisted we use our writing to think more deeply about ourselves and the world around us because it would make us happier, healthier people.

The abstract nature of poetry is one of the reasons researchers believe it can be so effective in helping us to express and understand our emotions. That is because poetry isn't necessarily literal. A poem about a storm may really be about a conflict in the poet's life. The storm becomes a metaphor for that experience. This allows the writer the freedom to express his emotions without violating the private nature of the relationship. For events that are too painful to face directly, the abstraction of poetry allows us to transfer our emotions to a less volatile subject and perhaps come to terms with them gradually.

Amina*

When I was teaching college I had an evening literature and composition class of primarily older adults with just a few teenagers/twentysomethings. One of the younger students was a quiet girl named Amina who had recently moved from Saudi Arabia. As I often do, I asked students in the course to keep a journal and to use it to respond to what they read. We had just finished a short story by an American writer about a westerner's negative experience in a strict Islamic society, and some of the class expressed negative views about the Middle Eastern society's values and the treatment of women.

Amina listened without participating in the discussion, but in her journal that night she wrote a poem. It was about a flower that grew well in the desert but was choked by weeds when it was transplanted to a greener climate. In her poem, there was a safety in the barren environment that was lost in the teeming plenty of the temperate one. It was evident that the flower was a metaphor for Amina herself, and that far from feeling freed by the openness of American society, she felt overwhelmed and even strangled by her new environment. Interestingly, the next time the class read a piece with a similar theme to the earlier story, she was quick to engage in the conversation and advocate for her native culture. I think writing the poem helped her to understand and better articulate her feelings.

The use of comparisons like similes and metaphors is called figurative language. While we use some figurative language in almost all of our writing, it is especially important in poetry. Poetry is language condensed to its essence. Because it is more compact than prose, every word you write—and every one you don't write—takes on increased meaning. You can't afford to waste words in a poem. We've all heard the saying "A picture is worth a thousand words," but a strong metaphor can create a picture in the mind of your reader using only a few words.

Look at the first two lines of Carl Sandburg's poem "Fog":

The fog comes
on little cat feet.

Seven words, but they create a vivid mental image through the use of metaphor. Sandburg taps into something we know—fog—and then makes us see it in a new way.

The poem above is unrhymed and follows no real pattern. Poems can adhere to a strict structure, like a sonnet or a haiku, or they can have no structure at all. Poets can use punctuation in every line, sparingly, or not at all. The common thread in poetry of every style is that every tool the poet chooses, whether it is a word, a capital letter, a comma or an empty space, has purpose and contributes to the meaning and impact of the poem as a whole.

In the following section, I've included some basic guidelines for writing poetry and some examples of a few types of short poems you might want to try. Remember that there is no "wrong way" to write a poem!

How To Write a Poem

There are two basic categories of poetry: lyric poetry and narrative poetry. The main purpose of lyric poetry is to share personal ideas, thoughts, and emotions. The main purpose of narrative poetry is to tell a story. Since expressive writing research has focused primarily on lyric poetry, that is the focus of these exercises.

Lyric poems can take many different forms, but no matter which one you choose to write, you can use the same basic process. All lyric poetry starts with images and ideas, so most poets do some form of brainstorming or free-writing to get those thoughts on paper. They then organize those thoughts into a specific poetic form.

Directions

1. **Brainstorm.**

    Your brainstorming can start with a "big idea," a single abstract concept like love or hate, or you can choose conflicting concepts (birth and death, joy and sorrow, creation and destruction). You can also start with a concrete object or experience and let the "big idea" develop as you write.

1-A Big Idea Brainstorm
- Choose a topic from the list or create one of your own.
- Write the topic in a circle in the center of a blank page. You can use Template A as a model.
- What words or phrases come to mind first when you look at the word/words? Write them on the map.
- Are there any objects that remind you of this topic? Why?

How does each look, feel, smells, taste, sound?
- Does your topic remind you of any incident from your own life? Add these to your map.

1-B Object or Place Brainstorm
- Choose a topic from the list or create one of your own.
- Write the topic in a circle in the center of a blank page. You can use Template A as a model.
- Look at or imagine the object or place you have chosen. Examine and experience it through your senses. Write what you see, smell, taste, touch, and hear on your map.
- Does your topic remind you of something else? How or why? Add it to your brainstorming.
- What emotions do you feel while brainstorming? Add them to your map.

2. **Choose a form.**

    Look over the types of lyric poetry described at the end of this chapter. Choose the one that you feel best fits your topic, brainstorming, and the kind of writing you like to do.

3. **Sift through your brainstorming.**

    Once you have an idea of the type of poem you want to write and its length, read over your brainstorming map. Highlight or circle the strongest thoughts, ideas, and images. Rewrite those on another page.

4. **Organize your thoughts.**

    Look at the lines you have kept. How are they connected? Do they show a single emotion or mood, or do they show more than one? If you are writing a poem with more than one stanza, experiment with dividing your lines into groups. If you are writing a haiku, choose the strongest image or images you have that represent a single emotion. If you are writing a diamante, consider choosing two groups of lines that evoke different emotions or themes.

5. **Form a poem.**

Rewrite the lines you've chosen in a rough poetic form. If you want to follow a specific rhyme scheme, syllable count, or rhythm, you can:

- cross out words that don't add to meaning, like a, an, the, very, too, and so
- add or remove suffixes like -ing or -ed
- substitute words that fit better or paint a more vivid picture but still have the same meaning

Remember, you don't have to follow a specific pattern. The purpose is to write out your thoughts and feelings. If you think your poem is finished, then it is.

Poem Starters

Big Ideas

- Love
- Hate
- Jealousy
- Anger
- Joy
- Sorrow
- Greed
- Caring
- Betrayal
- Death
- Birth
- Old Age
- Childhood
- Adolescence
- Family

Everyday Objects

A pet toy
- The kitchen table
- A pillow
- The doorbell
- The mailbox
- Your hand
- A wedding ring
- An empty glass
- A baby's shoe
- An unopened letter
- A cookbook
- A photograph

Places

- Your porch
- The garden
- Main street in a small town
- A church
- The beach
- A graveyard
- Your childhood home
- A hospital waiting room
- A baby shower
- A homeless shelter
- The woods in autumn
- A car on a dark highway

Conflicting Concepts

- Love/Hate
- Creation/Destruction
- Trust/Suspicion
- Lies/Truth
- Hope/Despair
- Joy/Sorrow
- Anger/Forgiveness
- Life/Death
- Bravery/Cowardice

Short Poetic Forms

The Haiku

A haiku is a short Japanese poetic form. It is meant to capture a single image or moment in time, and often focuses on nature. A haiku has only three lines, with a set syllable count (or number of beats) of 5-7-5.

Orange sun rising
Splashing colors pink and red
Against gray canvas

Notice that the poem doesn't tell about the sunrise but rather shows, using vivid language and a metaphor of the sun as a painter.

The Diamante or Diamond Poem

This is a seven-line poem in the shape of a diamond. It usually describes two contrasting or conflicting ideas and does not use rhyme.

youth
raw bold
stretching, changing, rebelling
dreaming the future, dreaming the past
shrinking, waiting, remembering
fragile whispered
age

The diamante follows this basic pattern:

Line 1: Beginning subject

Line 2: Two describing words about line 1

Line 3: Three doing words about line 1 ending with ing

Line 4: A short phrase about line 1, a short phrase about line 7

Line 5: Three doing words line 7

Line 6: Two describing words about line 7

Line 7: End subject

The Couplet

Just as its name suggests, a couplet is two lines of poetry, usually rhyming. A couplet can be a stand-alone poem, or you can write a series of related couplets as stanzas for a longer poem.

> *She rocks with a fierce energy, eyes pinned to the dark street*
> *Watching for the line of soldiers, listening for booted feet.*

The Quatrain

This is a four-line poem in which the second and fourth lines rhyme. It usually has a rhythm created by a pattern of stressed and unstressed syllables similar to a nursery rhyme.

> *Snow falls soft and silent*
> *On a new dug grave*
> *Melted by hot tears*
> *For the wife he couldn't save.*

If you want to write a longer poem, you can write several related quatrains as stanzas. If you choose, you can begin with three quatrains and end with a rhyming couplet, and you've written a sonnet!

The Acrostic Poem

Rhyming or unrhyming, the acrostic gets its name from the fact that the first letter of each line, when read vertically, forms a word related to the poem's theme or topic.

Healing does not come at once, not here, he says
Only in fairytales where wizards work their magic
Patient suffering is the key to our survival
Even the dog knows that

The Free Verse Poem

This is the most unstructured of poems, with no set length, rhyme, or rhythmic pattern. The words can be arranged on the page in any way you choose.

The moonlight reaches her long fingers across our bed

To caress your brow

You stir and say a word my name or hers

Or the name of the cold white light

We are all one to you

9

Opinions, Advice,

& the God Perspective

I was telling myself the story of a life, and this transmutes into an adventure the things which can shatter you.

Anaïs Nin

Secrets of the Writers' Club

I was having lunch a few months ago with a table full of writers. Our little group included a poet, a romance novelist, two children's book authors, a mystery writer, a woman who wrote DIY e-books, and an author of very successful young adult sci-fi and (believe it or not) adult erotica. All were published, and all had a personal history of creative writing that went back decades. When we went around the table to share our current projects, I was hesitant to discuss the research I was doing on *The Writing Prescription*. These women were already writers—I didn't think they would find a book about the power of writing particularly interesting.

I was wrong.

The poet greeted the idea enthusiastically. Writing, she said, is what kept her sane. The romance novelist shared that writing was what got her through the death of her husband. One of the children's book authors credited her writing with giving her life new direction. All of them agreed that the very act of writing made them happier, apart from any money they made from doing it.

Writing fiction is not that different from writing non-fiction. As writers, we use bits and pieces of our lives and the people we've known, and combine them to tell a story about the human condition. In doing so, we must think deeply, reflect on ourselves and our experiences, and consider the perspectives of others. It is no surprise, then, that all of the women in the writers' group felt they owed a debt to their writing. Without meaning to, all of us were following the research recommendations for improving our happiness and health through writing.

This made me reflect on the first writing I did professionally—a humorous magazine article for a boating magazine. I wrote about how my husband and I had developed hand signals to use in high stress situations like rough weather or docking. Titled "Stop Yelling at Me," it was as much about negotiating relationships as it was about boating. I wrote it when I was feeling useless and depressed, a mood I couldn't shake that was starting to affect my marriage. Through the act of writing I found purpose and an outlet for my negative emotions. Of course, it didn't hurt that it was accepted by an editor and I got my first check with my name on it—but the real uptick in my attitude came from the writing itself, not the money or the praise that followed.

Think back to the PTSD study. The veterans who participated in the writing groups showed some improvement regardless of whether they wrote with great emotion. Perhaps any time we put pen to paper thoughtfully, no matter the purpose, we resolve something within.

Creative non-fiction covers a broad range of writing. Anything based on fact or actual events is considered non-fiction, from DIY advice to memoirs. What makes it creative is the use of the same techniques --like humor, exaggeration, figurative language, or multiple perspectives—already used by storytellers and poets. The exercises in this chapter have been divided into three groups, opinion, advice, and narrative essays, but all three have elements in common.

The Creative Non-Fiction Smorgasbord

Opinion Essays

In an opinion essay, the writer takes one side of a controversial or contested issue and supports it. That doesn't mean the writer ignores the point of view of the opposition; in fact, it is important to consider that point of view when forming an argument. You must defend your views against the opposing evidence, so that evidence must be addressed in your own supporting information. When possible, use anecdotes from your own experience or that of someone you know. A strong personal voice is the most persuasive. Opinion essays can be serious, humorous, or a combination of both.

While you may choose to write only for yourself, depending on your topic there are many potential audiences for opinion essays. Local newspapers and magazines often have an editorial section and welcome contributions from the community. If you have a cause you believe in passionately, you might consider writing an opinion essay to support it.

How-To Essay

Do you have some wisdom you'd like to share? Perhaps it is a skill you've acquired by trial and error, and you'd like to save your son or daughter the trouble of figuring it out on their own. Perhaps it is a method of living that has made you happier or has led to a more successful marriage. Like the opinion essay, this piece can be humorous and/or serious, as long as it focuses on explaining some kind of process or procedure.

Some how-to essays are written to be shared. (You are reading one right now!) Others are written for the writer, often to clarify mistakes or misconceptions and analyze other steps that might have proven beneficial.

Narrative Essays: A New Perspective

All of the expressive writing exercises you've read over to this point have been written in the first-person perspective—in other words, yours. Even when you are considering the thoughts and feelings of your intended audience, as in the chapter on letter-writing, it is still your voice that comes across in the writing. When you write a memoir about a particular event, all of the details come from your memory and perception of events. Have you ever wondered what the same experience would look like if you had the ability to read the thoughts of everyone present at the time? In literature this perspective is called third person omniscient, or "all knowing," and is sometimes referred to as "the God perspective." Imagine you as the writer are removed from a personal stake in the event, but instead are watching and seeing the event through every characters' eyes. When focusing on frightening or hurtful memories from childhood or adolescence, writing in the third person can provide some emotional distance from the memory. After all, it isn't the "you" of the present, but rather who you used to be. Matthew Anderson, author of a 2013 University of Iowa study into assuming a third person perspective in writing, explains:

"Taking an observer's vantage may be vital to maintaining composure and making progress when trying to sort through a distressing or angering event or moment in life. It's a short leap from picturing a difficult personal event from an observer's perspective to actually using a third-person pronoun, as if you're looking at a completely different person going through what you did."

Writing in the third person omniscient also forces the writer to get inside other people's heads, to imagine how they felt and what they were thinking, to try and understand how and why they behaved as they did. Things that would have been unfathomable to the child you were at the time may be completely reasonable when you think about them deeply from another's point of view.

Most narrative essays are not meant to be shared. Despite our best attempts, we do not have the ability to see inside of others, and it is likely our portrayal of others would be seen as inaccurate or worse. These narratives can be fictionalized, changing characters and altering events but leaving the root of the story. Many successful authors begin with the seed of an actual event and grow it into a short story or novel whose characters and plot bear only a passing resemblance to the original experience but still capture the lesson or message it conveyed to them. Whether you choose to use your narrative as the basis for a fictional piece or simply write it for your self-growth and discovery, it will open up new insights into your past and your relationships.

How to Write a Creative Non-Fiction Essay

The Opinion Essay

Directions:

1. **Choose one of the topics below.**

   Topics with Humor
   - Why you should/should not vacation by a nude beach
   - Why you should/should not post on *Facebook* while drinking wine
   - Why you should/should not go online shopping while drinking wine
   - Why you should/should not interrogate your daughter's new boyfriend
   - Why you should/should not dress your age
   - Why you should/should not tell the truth on dating sites

   Topics with a Serious Side
   - Why you should/should not adopt a pet
   - Why you should/should not invite your in-laws to move in
   - Why you should/should not believe everything you read
   - Why you should/should note vote for _____
   - Why you should/should not have your phone out in restaurants
   - Why you should/should not support the current legislation/proposal about _____

2. Write an essay of three or more paragraphs sharing your opinion about the topic. Your essay should have an introduction that catches the reader's attention, examples that support your opinion, and a conclusion that reinforces your point.

After Writing

3. Read over your essay. Is there anything you wrote that surprises you now that you have read over it? Did your feelings change at all from the time you chose your topic to the time you finished writing? How do you think a reader will respond to your essay?

4. Think about the writing itself. Is your point of view clearly supported? Did you think of opposing arguments and try to counter them? Did you present your support in a way that was creative, original, or entertaining? Is there anything you could change to make your essay more convincing?

The How-To Essay

Directions:

1. **Choose one of the topics below.**

    Topics with Humor
    - How to remember your anniversary (and other essential information)
    - How to ride a motorcycle over age 70
    - How to eat dessert and stay skinny
    - How to survive a zumba class
    - How to create the perfect man cave
    - How to avoid household chores
    - How to aggravate your family member without getting caught
    - How to be a happy shopoholic

Topics with a Serious Side
- How to fight in a marriage
- How to survive a divorce
- How to stay positive when battling _____
- How to fall in love again
- How to let the past go
- How to forgive
- How to discipline with love
- How to keep going when you want to quit

2. Write an essay of three or more paragraphs explaining how to do the activity. Your essay should have an introduction that states your purpose, clear steps or a detailed process to complete the task, and a conclusion. Use language to create a tone that is appropriate to your topic.

After Writing

3. Read over your essay. Is there anything you wrote that surprises you now that you have read over it? Did your feelings change at all from the time you chose your topic to the time you finished writing? How do you think a reader will respond to your essay?

4. Think about the writing itself. Do you present enough clear advice/information for your reader to follow? Is everything explained in a detailed way? Did you include enough of your own thoughts and feelings to make your advice compelling? Is there anything you could add or change to make your essay more effective?

The Narrative Essay

Directions:

1. Go back to the Memoir Exercises on page 76. Choose one of these events and imagine you are an invisible observer with the ability to read the thoughts and feelings of everyone present. Using Template B, Storyboard Brainstorming as a guide, create a general outline of the events and the people involved. Treat yourself as just another named character in the story.

2. Using your outline, retell the story in paragraph form from the observer's point of view. Take your best guess as to what is motivating or driving each person's actions, what they are thinking, and how they feel. Try to stay as close to the actual events as possible and avoid judging any character's actions as good or bad, even your own.

After Writing

3. Read over your narrative essay. Did you come to any new conclusions about the event or the people involved? Do you see your own role in the same way as you did when you started? Did you develop any deeper understanding of what motivated you or others?

4. Does the narrative have a clear beginning, middle, and end? Did you tell the story in a fair and believable way? How do you think the other people involved would react to your re-telling of the story?

10

Resources: Templates, Glossaries

&

Other Tools of the Trade

The difference between the right word and the nearly right word is the same as the difference between lightning and the lightning bug.

Mark Twain

Template A – *Basic Mental Map/Brainstorming Web*

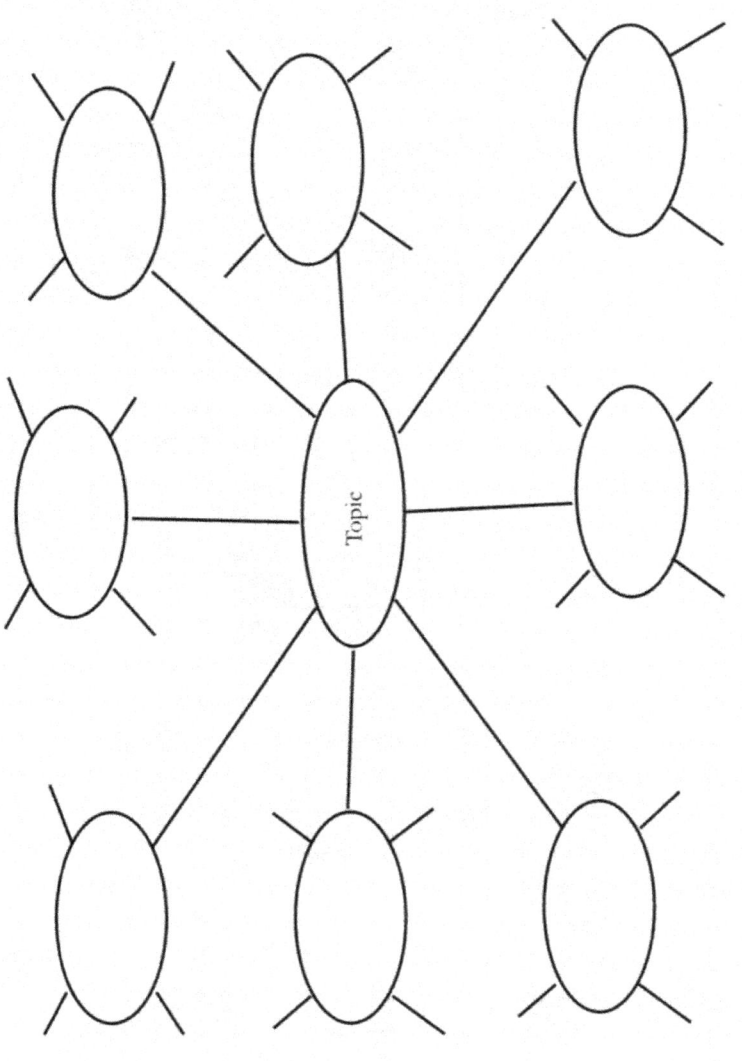

Template B – *Storyboard Brainstorming*

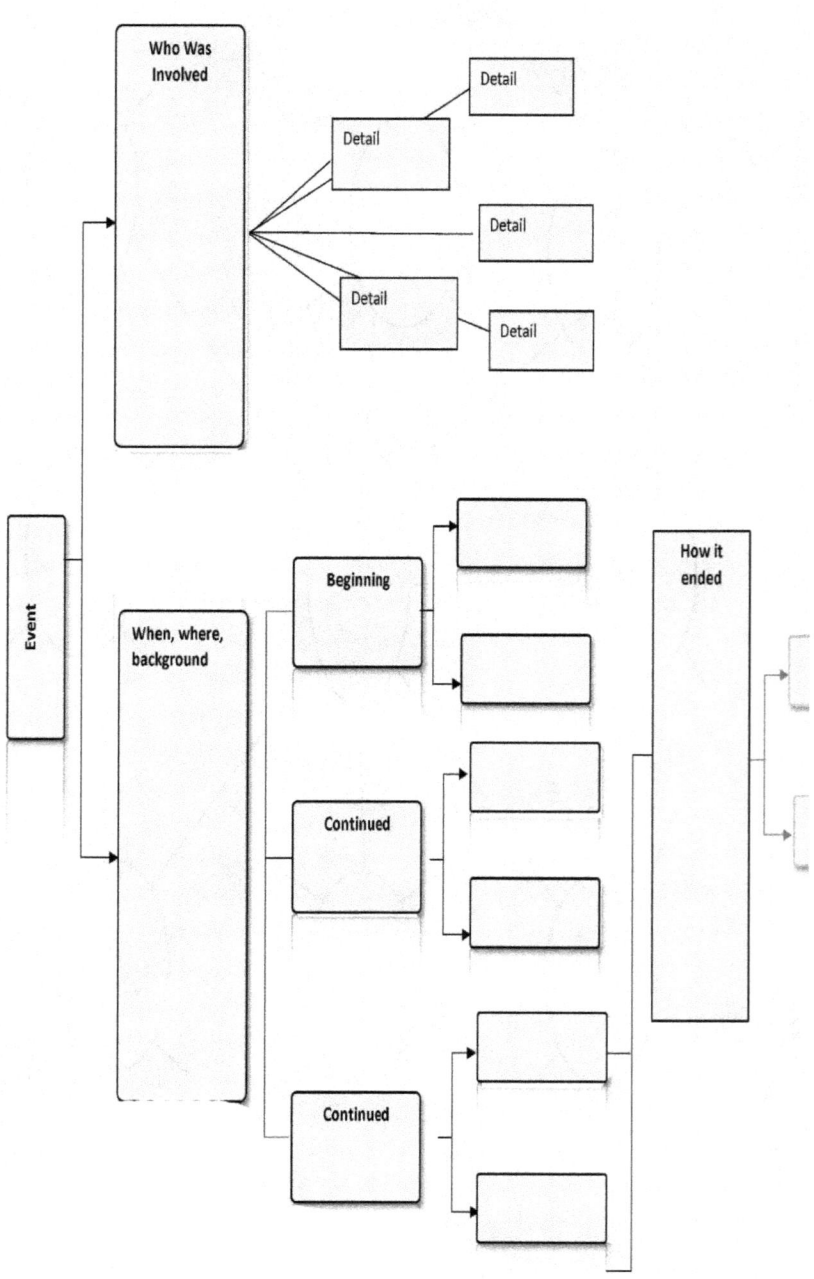

Glossary of Writing Terms

Term	Definition	Example
Alliteration	Using the same sound at the beginning of several words in a line	The soft smooth silk whispered against her skin.
Analogy	A comparison between two unlike things to make the reader see something unexpected. Similes and metaphors are types of analogies.	"We will not be satisfied until justice rolls down like waters, and righteousness like a mighty stream"—Martin Luther King, Jr.
Catharsis	A release of negative emotions as a result of the arts	Her catharsis came when she wrote about her father's death.
Cliché'	A word or phrase that has lost its impact through overuse	It rained cats and dogs.
Climax	The high point or turning point in a story	The climax of *Romeo and Juliet* came when Romeo entered the tomb.
End rhyme	Words with the same sound at the ends of lines of poetry	The girl cried To see he had died.
Hyperbole	Exaggeration to create an effect	His beard was unkempt and could have hidden a dozen birds' nests.

Term	Definition	Example
Imagery	The use of figurative language (such as metaphors and similes), sensory language, and sound devices in writing to create vivid mental pictures	The wounded snake slithered on the ground, its body writhing and undulating, leaving a trail of wet blood.
Metaphor	An analogy made directly, not using words such as like or as	Her hair fell in golden waves that crested on his chest.
Personification	Giving something non-human human characteristics	The rain tiptoed lightly across the tin roof.
Simile	An analogy made indirectly using words such as like or as	Her anger was like a force of nature, crashing down upon us.
Rhyme Scheme	A pattern of end rhyme; it can be described by assigning letters to words at the ends of lines, repeating letters when a rhyme occurs	Roses are red a Violets are blue, b Sugar is sweet c And so are you. d

Journaling:

List Prompts #2

1. Name five things you're proud of yourself for doing, even if no one else knew.
2. Name three things about yourself you'd like to work on.
3. List five things you could do next week to make someone else in your life happy.
4. Give examples of three good surprises you have had in your life.
5. List three things you'd like to do if you weren't afraid.
6. Imagine you had to evacuate your house quickly and could take only take three things. Tell what you would take with you.
7. List three skills you'd like to learn if you had the time.
8. List your five favorite date nights.
9. Name your four worst fears.
10. List your three most embarrassing moments.
11. List five things on your bucket list.
12. List five things you love about your spouse or significant other.
13. List four sights you want to see before you die.
14. Name the five people you would most like to talk to in heaven.
15. List five places/times from the past you'd like to visit.

Journaling:

List Prompts #2

1. Name five things you're proud of yourself for doing, even if no one else knew.
2. Name three things about yourself you'd like to work on.
3. List five things you could do next week to make someone else in your life happy.
4. Give examples of three good surprises you have had in your life.
5. List three things you'd like to do if you weren't afraid.
6. Imagine you had to evacuate your house quickly and could only take three things. Tell what you would take with you.
7. List three skills you'd like to learn if you had the time.
8. List your five favorite date nights.
9. Name your four worst fears.
10. List your three most embarrassing moments.
11. List five things on your bucket list.
12. List five things you love about your spouse or significant other.
13. List four sights you want to see before you die.
14. Name the five people you would most like to talk to in heaven.
15. List five places/times from the past you'd like to visit.

Free Writing Topics #2

Places

- A busy restaurant
- A boat on the water
- The middle of the woods
- Your favorite place to play as a child
- Your favorite hiding place

People

- Your first love
- A stranger whose eyes you met
- A waiter or waitress in the last place you ate
- The cashier in the last place you shopped
- A character from a book you love
- Yourself of ten, twenty, or thirty years ago
- Yourself ten, twenty, or thirty years in the future

Objects

- A pair of skates
- A musical instrument
- An egg in a nest
- A woman' scarf
- Your oldest piece of jewelry
- Your first car

Basic Journal Starters #2

1. Tell about something you did and regretted when you were younger. How do you feel about it now?
2. Do you believe there is a single soulmate for everyone?
3. Do you believe in love at first sight?
4. If you could go back and relive some portion of your life, would you? Why or why not?
5. If you could go back in time and apologize to someone, who would it be, and what would you apologize for?
6. If you could invent something to solve one problem, either personally or globally, what would it be?
7. What would you like people to notice about you the first time you meet?
8. Describe a time when you have been most frightened.
9. Would you rather be in a room full of people or alone?
10. What are you most grateful for in your life today?
11. Describe a time someone did something special for you.
12. Did you grow up in a religious household? How did your upbringing influence your belief in God?
13. Do you believe that animals have souls?
14. If you had to give up one food forever, which would be the hardest to part with?
15. Is it better to be smart or lucky?
16. Is it better to be beautiful or kind?

Bibliography

Adams, K. (2006). *Life stories for seniors*. Center for Journal Therapy, online.

Baikie, K. et al (2005). Emotional and physical health benefits of expressive writing. *Advances in Psychiatric Treatment*, 338-343.

Barry M. Staw, R. I. (1994). Employee positive emotion and favorable outcomes at the workplace. *Organization Science*, 51-71.

Brown University Long-Term Care Quality Advisor. (1997). Poetry is ageless. *The Later Years*.

Colino, S. (2016, August 16). Putting pen to paper, or fingers to keyboard, can really pay off. *U.S. News and World Report*.

Csikszentmihaly, M. et al (1991). Motivation and academic achievement: the effects of personality traits and the duality of experience. *Journal of Personality*, 539-574.

Diener, E. et al (2002). Very happy people. *Psychological Science*, 81-84.

Diener, E. S. (1995). Differences In Reported Well-Being. *Social Indicators Research*, 7-32.

Dooley, R. (2013). Print vs. digital: another emotional win for paper. *Neuromarketing*.

Emmons, R. A. (2003). counting blessings versus burdens: experimental studies of gratitude and subjective well-being in daily life. *Journal of Personality and Social Psychology*, 377-389.

Estrada, C. I. (1994). Positive affect influences creative problem solving and reported source of practice satisfaction in physicians. *Motivation and Emotion*. 285–299.

Fredrickson, B. L. (2001). The role of positive emotions in positive psychology: The broaden-and-build theory of positive emotions. *American Psychologist*, 218–226.

Freedman, J. (1978). *Happy People: What Happiness Is, Who Has It, and Why*. New York: Harcourt Brace Jovanovich.

Happiness improves health and lengthens life, review finds. (2011). *Science News*. Vol 331, Issue 6022

Harker, L. et al (2001). Expressions of positive emotions in women's college yearbook pictures and their relationship to personality and life outcomes across adulthood. *Journal of Personality and Social Psychology*, 112–124.

Hemies, S. M. (2011). State of poetry therapy. *Arts in Psychiatry, 108*.

Jolly, M. (2011) What I never wanted to tell you. *Journal of Medical Humanities* 32, 47-59

Koschwanez, H. K. (2013). Expressive writing and wound healing in older adults. *Psychosomatic Medicine*, 581-590.

Lyubomirsky, S. S. (2005). Pursuing happiness: the architecture of sustainable change. *Review of General Psychology*, 111–131.

Marks, G. N. (1999). Influences and consequences of well-being among Australian young people: 1980–1995. *Social Indicators Research*, 301–323.

Miklos, J. J. (2007). The power of poetry. *Reading Today*, online.

Okun, M. A. (1984). The social activity/subjective wellbeing relation: a quantitative synthesis. *Research on Aging*, 45–65.

Patel, R. R. (2015). *Study: Could Social Media Use Increase Depression*. Phio State University.

Pennebaker, J. W. (1997). Writing about emotional experiences as a therapeutic process. *Psychological Science*, 162–166.

Petrie, F. T. (2004). Effect of written emotional expression on immune function in patients with human immunodeficiency virus infection: a randomized trial. *Psychosomatic Medicine*, 272-275.

Rickett, C. G. (2011). Something to hang my life on: the health benefits of writing poetry for people with serious illnesses . *Australasian Psychiatry*, 265-268.

Routledge, C. P. (2014, June 23). Five scientifically supported benefits of prayer. *Psychology Today*.

Smyth, J. et al (2015). Writing about stressful experience reduces symptoms of asthma or rheumatoid arthritis. *The Journal of the American Osteopathic Association.* 1304-1309

Smyth, J. H. (2008). Expressive writing and post-traumatic stress disorder: effects on trauma symptoms, mood states, and cortisol reactivity. *British Journal of Health and Psychology*, 85-93.

Toepfer, S. et al (2009). Letters of gratitude: improving well-being through expressive writing. *Journal of Writing Research*, 181-198.

Watkins, P. C. (2003). Gratitude and happiness: Development of a measure of gratitude, and relationship with subjective well-being. *Social Behavior & Personality: An International Journal*, 431-452.

Index

A

A Big Idea Brainstorm

Acrostic Poem

Anaïs Nin 71, 95

Anne Flaxman 29

A Word About Online Journaling 49

B

Basic Journal Starters

Basic Journal Starters #1 59

behavioral improvements 37

brain-derived neurotrophic factor 16

Brandler, Sondra 28

Buckley, Michael 19

C

cancer patients 36

Carson, Shelley 31

Coler Goldwater Specialty Hospital & Nursing Facility 28

Couplet

Creative writing 31

D

Diamante Poem

Diary-style 57, 58

E

expressive letter writing 63

F

Facebook 3, 49, 102

Facetime 12

Free Verse Poem

Free Writing Topics

Free-Writing Topics 55

G

General Letter-Writing Directions: 66

Glossary of Writing Terms

Goldwater Writing Workshop 28

gratitude journals 26

Gratitude Letter 68

H

Haiku

Harvard University 31

Heimes, Silke 30

Historical Memoir 77

How to Journal 50

How to Write a Memoir 76

How to Write a Poem

I

I'm Sorry Letter 69

Intensive Journal Method 21

J

Jiyoung Park 73

Johnson, Samuel 61

Journaling

Journaling Lite: The List 50

L

Letter of Understanding 68
Letter to the Future 69
Lindbergh, Anne Morrow 39
List Journaling Prompts 52
List Prompts
Lutgendorf, Susan 48
Lyubomirsky, Sonja 15

M

Memoir 29, 30, 73, 74, 75, 78, 79, 100

N

Narrative Essays
New York University 28
New York University School of Social Work 28

P

Pennebaker, James 21, 46
Personal Memoir 76
Poem Starters
Power of Paper 38
Prayer 17, 26, 66
Progoff, Ira 21
Psychology Today 31
PTSD 36, 37, 98

Q

Quatrain

R

Reflective Response 46, 57, 58
Reflective Response Journaling 57
Rowling, J.K. 33

S

Shakespeare 12
Short Poetry Forms
Single Event Memoir 76
Skype 12
Spirituality 26

T

Thankfulness 26, 27
The Acrostic Poem
The Arts in Psychotherapy 30
The Center for Journal Therapy 29
The Diary 46
The Free Verse Poem
The Free-Write 53
The Golden Writers Anthology 28
The How-To Essay
The Multiple Event Memoir 79
The Narrative Essay
The Opinion Essay

U

Unfinished Business Letter 68
University of Auckland 36
University of Iowa 48, 100
University of Massachusetts–Amherst 73

W

What Letter Writing Won't Do 70

Z

Zinsse, William 73

About the Author

Ann Eichenmuller is the author of two novels—Kind Lies and The Lies We Are. She is an award-winning essayist and travel writer whose work has been featured in All at Sea, Chesapeake Style, Chesapeake Bay, and Motorhome magazines.

A former Maryland educator, she received the Washington Post's Agnes Meyer Award for Excellence. She has a B.A. in English and an M.A. in Humanities.

Ann is a certified diver, private pilot, and something of an adventurer who counts sailing her boat to the Bahamas with husband Eric and their children as her favorite accomplishment.

Other books by Ann Eichenmuller

Kind Lies
The Lies We Are

Publisher's Note

We want to acknowledge the readers who read and commented on the advance review copies of *The Writing Rx*:

Jane Park Cutler (MSW, PhD) grew up in Tennessee and worked in Georgia, Illinois, Virginia, Indiana, and Maryland at various social service departments, nonprofit organizations and universities, as well as a private practice as a therapist. While she loved her career, her greatest joy is her husband and their two children Elizabeth (in Paris) and Clark (in San Francisco). Happily, after a career of thirty some years in the social work profession, she was able to take an early retirement and moved to Deltaville on the Chesapeake Bay where she and her husband enjoy sailing on *Tender Mercies*.

Sharon Canfield Dorsey is an award-winning author and poet. She is Vice President-Eastern Division for the Virginia Poetry Society. She is a member of Pen Women International, James City Poets and the Chesapeake Bay Writers. Dorsey has received awards from the CNU Writers Conference, Poetry Society of Virginia, Gulf Coast Writer's Association and Chesapeake Bay Writers.She was a 2017 winner of the Art Lit project to display poetry on the sidewalks of the city of Williamsburg. Dorsey is the author of two children's books, *Herman the Hermit Crab and the Mystery of the Big, Black, Shiny Thing*; and *Revolt of the Teacups*; a memoir, *Daughter of the Mountains*; and a book of poetry, *Tapestry*. Her poems are also included in an anthology by the James City Poets, titled, *Captured Moments*. She is a senior sales director of 38 years with Mary Kay Cosmetics, mom to son, Steven and daughter, Shannon, and grandmother to Adaline, Emma and Zachary.

Cindy L. Freeman is a award-winning author who writes about the difficulties women face in challenging relationships. Cindy lives in Williamsburg, Virginia where she directed a music school for twenty-six years before retiring. Her books *Unrevealed, The Dark Room* and *Diary in the Attic* are available on Amazon.com. She has two children and five grandchildren.

Michael S. Glaser (PhD) served as Poet Laureate of Maryland from 2004 –2009. He is a Professor Emeritus at St. Mary's College of Maryland where he served as both a professor of English and an administrator for nearly 40 years. While at St. Mary's, he co-founded the annual Literary Festival as well as the VOICES literary reading series. A recipient of the Homer Dodge Endowed Award for Excellence in Teaching, the Columbia Merit Award from the Poetry Committee of the Greater Washington, D.C. area, and Loyola College's Andrew White Medal for his dedication to the intellectual and scholarly life. Widely sought as a speaker and workshop leader, Glaser served as a Maryland State Arts Council poet-in-the-schools for over 25 years. He is the author of several books of poetry, including *Being a Father, Fire Before Hands,* and *A Lover's Eye,* and *Remembering Eden.*

Beverly Peterson (PhD) taught classes in literature, composition, and English as a Second Language at the middle school, high school, and college levels for over forty years. She earned her BA and MA in English and her PhD in American Studies from the College of William and Mary. After retiring from her much-loved tenured job at Penn State Fayette, she returned to Williamsburg where she delighted in teaching for seven years at her Alma Mater.